S0-AEC-096

DISCARDED

DISCARDED

Ancient Peoples and Places

S I C I L Y

General Editor

DR GLYN DANIEL

DR GLYN DANIEL *Ancient Peoples and Places*

SICILY

BEFORE THE GREEKS

L. Bernabò Brea

78 PHOTOGRAPHS
50 LINE DRAWINGS
AND 7 MAPS

Upsala College
Library
East Orange, N. J.

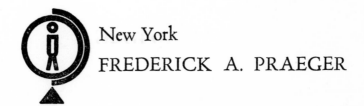

New York
FREDERICK A. PRAEGER

BOOKS THAT MATTER

Published in the United States of America
in 1957 by Frederick A. Praeger, Inc.,
Publishers, 150 East 52nd Street,
New York 22, N.Y.

All rights reserved

Library of Congress Catalog Card Number: 57-12973

Printed in Great Britain

913.378
B 828 s

64526

To V. Gordon Childe

CONTENTS

7

CONTENTS

ILLUSTRATIONS

Acknowledgements

Many people have facilitated my researches, both by their kindness or by their active contribution to the preparation of this book. I would specially thank Signora Iole Marconi Bovio, Soprintendente alle Antichità in Palermo, Dottore Giovanni Rizza of the University of Catania, Mlle Madeleine Cavalier of the Lipari Museum, Signor Santo Tinè of the Soprintendenza alle Antichità of Syracuse, and many others. I would also like to express my gratitude to Signor Salvatore Fontana of the Syracuse Museum, and to Professor Oreste Puzzo and Signor Uberto Lazzarini, draughtsmen in the same museum, for their collaboration in preparing the illustrations for this work; also to Signor Luigi Guido and Miss C. M. Preston for the help they have given me, over and above the work of translating.

MAP I Sicily and the Central Mediterranean Region

Introduction

THE ORIGINAL RESEARCHES on the prehistory of Sicily were made by geologists, and it is because of this that the palaeolithic cultures were studied before the neolithic ones.

The first deposits to attract scholarly attention were the numerous caves on the Palermo and Trapani coasts, particularly rich in remains of extinct fauna, and their systematic exploration was started by Falconer as early as 1859. His work was continued by Baron Francesco Anca, and later, from 1866 onwards, by G. G. Gemellaro. At the same time Marquis Dalla Rosa first explored the caves of the Trapani littoral and the island of Favignana, and Saverio Ciofalo did the same in the Termini Imerese neighbourhood. The first general picture of Sicilian prehistory was made by Baron F. von Andrian in 1878.

The historians and archaeologists make a much later appearance than the naturalists: attracted above all by the extreme richness of the classical remains, they continued for many years to base their knowledge of pre-Greek Sicily on the interpretation of the historical data and legends handed down by the ancient writers.

For some time the only result of archaeological research was that the rock-tombs in the vast East Sicilian cemeteries were attributed by Schubring and Cavallari to the indigenous Sikels.

A new era began, however, for studies in prehistoric archaeology from the time when Paolo Orsi started his devoted career of excavation and research in Sicily. Born at Rovereto near Trento, he joined the museum at Syracuse in 1888 as an assistant to F. S. Cavallari; a few years later he succeeded to the directorship of the museum, to which he was to dedicate all his life until his death in 1935. Orsi is the great discoverer of prehistoric Sicily, as also of Christian and Byzantine Sicily. With untiring activity and very methodically he began the exploration of its countryside, and the systematic excavation of all the main archaeological and prehistoric centres. In a short time he made the Syracuse Museum into one of the greatest museums in Italy.

In the space of only five years, between 1890 and 1895, he explored Stentinello, the cemeteries of Melilli, Castelluccio, Plemmyrion, Molinello, Finocchito, Thapsos, Cozzo del Pan⁄tano, all not far from Syracuse. As early as 1892 he established his classification of the four 'Siculan' periods, preceded by a Neolithic period (Stentinello) to which he later added an intermediate sixth period represented by the San Cono⁄Piano Notaro culture. His classification still remains valid in its main outlines, even if the results of subsequent research, including some of his own, make it possible for us today to reconstruct a richer and more complex picture of prehistoric Sicily than he was able to do.

In the following decades he extended his activities to cover an increasingly wide area, including the districts of Catania, Caltagirone, Gela, Agrigento, and finally Messina and even Calabria. The immensity of his task both as an excavator and as guardian of the vast archaeological wealth from such a large territory as the whole of Sicily and Calabria left him no time, after he had made a thorough survey of each exploration, to synthesize his work of about half a century.

That synthesis was attempted by others: first in 1904–5 by Giuseppe Angelo Colini in the *Bollettino di Paletnologia Italiana*, then in 1925 by the brothers Corrado and Ippolito Cafici in an article of fundamental importance in *Reallexikon der Vorgeschichte*. Peet, Patroni and Pace, on their part, dealt with the problems of Sicilian prehistory in works of a more general character.

The Cafici brothers are, after Orsi, the two main contributors to our knowledge of prehistoric archaeology in eastern Sicily; Corrado threw much light on the Neolithic in Sicily through his investigation of the villages of the Stentinello *facies* in the Etna region; Ippolito, through his very long scientific activity over seventy years, not only added to our knowledge of the Neolithic period, but he also discovered the working sites and the Campignian industry in Sicily.

Activity was less intensive in western and northern Sicily, where the work started by Antonino Salinas was carried on by Ettore Gabrici, Pirro Marconi, P. Mingazzini, P. E. Arias, P. Griffo and finally by Iole Marconi Bovio, to whom we owe not only a conspicuous series of field explorations, and the illustration of the Conca d'Oro culture, but also the discovery of the palaeolithic art of Sicily through the explorations of the Addaura and Niscemi caves, which followed very shortly after the discovery of the Levanzo *graffiti* illustrated by P. Graziosi.

These brilliant revelations gave new life to the interest in Sicilian palaeolithic studies which, after a remarkable start, passed through a period of comparative neglect for about fifty years. They were first resumed in 1928 by Ramond Vaufrey, who carried them on from the stage in which von Andrian had left them in 1878, through his excavations of the Mangiapane and San Teodoro caves, and through his systematic reexamination of all the material so far known.

Vaufrey's work was continued in the San Teodoro cave by C. Maviglia and P. Graziosi, who found there the first tombs and the first human remains belonging to this early period.

With the Lipari excavations, started in 1950, the Aeolian Islands were the latest to enter the field of Sicilian prehistory, but they immediately took a leading position. These excavations have provided the stratigraphical basis which had not been available before. They have not only enabled us to make a reconstruction of the cultural succession, especially for the

Neolithic and Copper Age, but they have also opened up new horizons in our knowledge of the relationships between east and west during the prehistoric periods.

Although much research has already been carried out in Sicilian prehistory during the last hundred years or so, a great deal still remains to be done. In some parts of the island the field work has not been so intensive or as complete as in others. Hitherto the finds plotted on a map of prehistoric Sicily reflect the distribution of research workers more than that of the various objects or sites. The find spots are in fact most densely grouped round Syracuse and Palermo, where the presence of the big national museums has not only facilitated intensive research but has also allowed a continuous supervision over chance discoveries to be maintained. Elsewhere there are very large areas where not a single find has been recorded, because no one has so far explored them scientifically. Moreover, as soon as an archaeologist takes on such a work, a piece of country archaeologically unknown suddenly reveals very rich remains of all epochs. This has happened, or is still happening, for example, in the Gela area through the work of Dinu Adamesteanu, in the Milazzo area through that of D. Ryolo, and in the Lipari Islands as a result of my own research and that of Mlle Cavalier.

It is therefore premature to try to find any connexion between the distribution of habitation sites and the geographical conditions of individual regions of the island; or any connexion between these sites and the surface geology, even if certain fundamental facts such as, for instance, the density of palaeolithic sites in the littoral caves between Palermo and Trapani, and of Castelluccio sites and cemeteries in south-eastern Sicily, or Conca d'Oro type tombs around Palermo seem to be very evident in the light of present knowledge.

On the other hand, we must acknowledge that in this respect even a preliminary serious study still remains to be carried out.

Rather, therefore, than try to survey the over-all distribution of the prehistoric cultures in Sicily, which would inevitably result in a most uneven picture and also for this reason be misleading, we prefer to examine the individual factors of a geographical character gradually in the course of our analysis of the various Aeolian and Sicilian cultural *facies*.

One of the difficulties we meet in attempting to co-ordinate the prehistoric evolution of Sicily with that of other regions farther to the east or west of the Mediterranean lies in the question of terminology.

Prehistoric studies in the eastern Mediterranean and in western Europe have hitherto been carried out to some extent independently of one another, and the same terms have had quite different connotations in the two areas. Sicily, a con-necting link between these two worlds, has close contacts with both. The problem therefore arose as to which of the two terminologies should be followed.

One single example will make this clear. The Sicilian Castelluccio culture and the coeval Capo Graziano culture of the Aeolian Islands, on the one hand, show contacts with the advanced stages of the Middle Helladic or the inception of the Late Helladic (i.e. with the cultures which are classified in the Aegean as Middle or Late Bronze Age); on the other hand, they received the bell-beakers which in the Iberian peninsula, southern France and northern Italy are regarded as characteristic of the Copper Age (or, according to more recent classifications, of Early Bronze Age I).

In the classification of the Sicilian cultures we have preferred to follow a middle course which seems to correspond best to the geographical position and cultural function of Sicily in the Mediterranean. While we have classified as Neolithic those cultures related to the Neolithic A and B of Greece, we have relegated to the Copper Age those cultures which show con-tacts with Neolithic Gamma and those corresponding to the

Upsala College
Library
East Orange, N. J.

21

Early Helladic, since it is difficult to draw any clear distinction between these, at least in eastern Sicily.

The Sicilian and Aeolian cultures, starting respectively with the Castelluccio and Capo Graziano cultures, have been treated here as belonging to the true Bronze Age, and the successive evolution of cultures in both places has been divided into Early, Middle and Late Bronze Age, in conformity with the cultural breaks which seem to be obvious both in Sicily and in the Aeolian Islands.

These divisions, in fact, seem to be far less valid in north-western Sicily; here the evolution, as we shall see, proceeded along different lines from that of eastern Sicily and the Aeolian Islands, where the cultural breaks seem so far to be much less evident.

CHAPTER I

The Palaeolithic and the Mesolithic

I. THE PALAEOLITHIC

THE ARRIVAL OF MAN seems to have been very late in Sicily. In fact, up till now no traces of Man have been found there belonging either to the Lower or Middle Palaeolithic period; that is to say, to those earliest human cultures which took up by far the greater part of the Pleistocene Age, and lasted until half-way through the Würm glaciation, the last of the four great glaciations characterizing this geological period. Perhaps it was not until then that Man crossed the Straits of Messina and penetrated into the island.

The Upper Palaeolithic stations so far identified in Sicily are very numerous, and some of them present us with great richness of material. Moreover, we must remember that large parts of the island still remain to be explored.

Until a short time ago—that is to say, until 1928, when Vaufrey wrote his admirable synthesis of the Palaeolithic of Italy—one had the impression that the Upper Palaeolithic cultures only flourished along the northern coasts of the island. The known stations extended in fact all along the coast from Termini Imerese to Trapani, and on the island of Favignana, which, in the Würmian period, must still have been joined to Sicily. The cave-site of San Teodoro, though still on the northern coast, was isolated from the main group and much nearer to Messina. All these stations were caves in the cliffs of ancient shore lines.

Only during the last few years has it been possible to identify a group of sites, belonging to this period, on the south-eastern point of Sicily, between Syracuse and Marina di Ragusa. Some of these Syracusan sites are situated on the uplands and may be as much as twenty-five miles from the sea. Some day, probably, new and more accurate field work will lead to the discovery of other stations. Some will possibly be in parts of the country from which, today at all events, the Upper Palaeolithic seems to be absent. Nevertheless, while not wishing to draw conclusions from *ex silentio* arguments, the coastal distribution prevailing in the Sicilian Palaeolithic seems well attested up to now.

Between the stations we have noted, sometimes even between those relatively close to one another, the industries often show very considerable typological differences. These differences might be mistaken for variations between one locality and another, whereas it is more probable that they reflect a difference in date.

So far not one of these stations has provided us with a stratified sequence of cultures, and it is thus impossible to establish their relative chronology. One can only try to do so by making typological comparisons with the known cultures from other, more distant, regions. In all these Sicilian sites, in fact, the stratigraphical conditions are the same: the culture level, of varying thickness, overlies a deposit of clay which, though rich in remains of fauna, is devoid of objects of human manufacture.

Vaufrey has demonstrated that these clay deposits which form the lowest stratum of the filling in Sicilian caves belong to the first part of the Würmian glaciation, i.e. to the period when the Mousterian culture was flourishing on all the other shores of the Mediterranean.

The fauna contained in these clay deposits that have no human industry in them is very interesting. Here one finds a quaternary fauna of a warm type which, owing to the southern latitude of Sicily, was able to survive even through the Glacial period. It is a fauna with big *Pachidermi* in which the hippopotamus (*Hippopotamus amphibius pentlandi*) was common, though the rhinoceros (*Rhinoceros merki*) was rare.

But the most characteristic element in this fauna complex is the dwarf elephant which Sicily had in common with the other Mediterranean islands (Sardinia, Crete and Cyprus), and above all with Malta, to which Sicily was certainly joined, at least until the beginning of the Pleistocene.

These dwarf elephants are descended from the biggest of the known elephants, the *Elephas antiquus*. Amongst them there can be recognized, chiefly on the basis of progressive dwarfism, three main varieties: *El. ant. mnaidrensis*, *El. ant. melitensis* and *El. ant. falconeri*. This last type can hardly have been larger than a big dog. These *pachidermi* are associated with lions and cave hyenas (*Felis leo spelaeus* and *Hyaena crocuta spelaea*), but the big cave bear is not found. Other species include a zebrated equid now extinct (*Equus (Asinus) hydruntinus* or Otranto horse), giant dormouse (*Myoxus (Leithia) melitensis*), wild horse (*Equus caballus*), bison (*Bison priscus*), an early species of ox (*Bos taurus primigenius*), red deer (*Cervus elaphus*), doe (*Cervus dama*), wild boar (*Sus scropha ferus*), brown bear (*Ursus arctos*), wolf (*Canis lupus*), fox (*Vulpes vulgaris*), hare (*Lepus europaeus*), etc.

It is a fauna in which specifically African elements are absent, and this argues against the original existence of a Siculo-African land-bridge during the Quaternary period.

But Man never saw this typical fauna of the Sicilian Pleistocene, for by the time he came to Sicily it had already, probably for a long time, been extinct. Only one of the great Quaternary mammals, now extinct, was still surviving, the *Equus (Asinus) hydruntinus*. To judge from the remains of this animal found amongst the food refuse, it must have been extensively hunted by palaeolithic man.

From the upper levels containing a human industry the fauna is a common one and comprises a considerably smaller number of species than that existing in the preceding period (wild horse, wild boar, red deer, *Bos primigenius*, fox, hare, etc.). But the enormous quantities of sea-shells, especially of large limpets (*Patella ferruginea*) which are found in most of these Sicilian Palaeolithic sites, show that the collection of molluscs along the shore for food was of great importance to the cave-dwellers, and that together with fishing, hunting and the picking of wild fruit it formed a basic part of the economy in this period.

From a typological point of view the earliest of the palaeo-lithic stations in Sicily is probably the small rock-shelter of Fontana Nuova near Marina di Ragusa, which, despite the absence of a bone industry, seems to belong to the true Middle Aurignacian, i.e. to a relatively early phase in the Upper Palaeolithic. The so-called back-blades which constitute the greater number of the worked implements in the Sicilian stations are here completely absent, as are also microlithic implements. Instead, we find types characteristic of the Aurig-nacian, like the notched blades with retouched edges, burins of Tarté type, or flat burins, and beaked scrapers. Also present are hand points, obliquely truncated blades with retouches along the truncation, and a variety of burins, including the *bec de flûte*, lateral and polyhedral types. Some blades with a prepared striking platform seem to be vaguely reminiscent of Mousterian techniques.

All the other Sicilian deposits, however, fall within the 'Gravettian' complex of industries which belong to a later date in the Upper Palaeolithic. The greater part of the instruments that characterize them are blades and points with battered backs, occasionally straight (i.e. of the classic La Gravette type), but more often curved, scrapers on the ends of blades, which may be either short or long, and discoidal scrapers. Along with these appear less frequently hand points and lateral points, knives of 'shell mound' type, small points, obliquely truncated blades, burin spalls, retouching flakes, etc. Among the burins the commonest type is the polyhedral or 'Romanelli' type, but sometimes *bec de flûte* or side burins are also found.

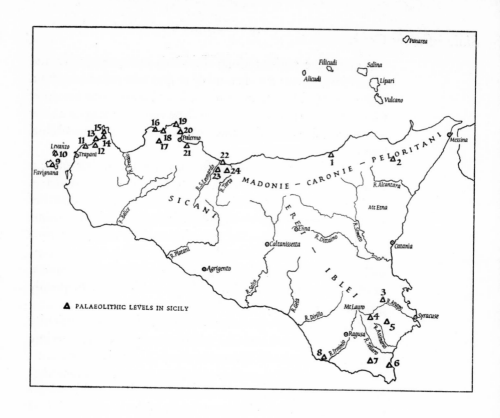

MAP II   Palaeolithic Levels in Sicily

1	San Teodoro	13	Crocifisso
2	San Basilio	14	Racchio
3	Sortino	15	Cala Mancina
4	Palazzolo Acreide	16	Puntali
5	Canicattini Bagni	17	Maccagnone
6	Grotta Corruggi	18	Carburanceli
7	Grotta Lazzaro	19	Grotta di Monte Gallo
8	Fontana Nuova	20	Addaura
9	Favignana	21	San Ciro
10	Levanzo	22	Castello di Termini Imerese
11	Grotta Emiliana	23	Natale
12	Mangiapane (Scurati)	24	Di Nuovo

27

Among the stations along the north coast, the larger and coarser implements are often made of quartzite rather than flint. There are notable variations in the *facies* between one station of Gravettian type and another, and these variations suggest a slow and progressive evolution towards more definitely 'microlithic' forms.

Some of these stations, as for instance the shelter of San Corrado at Palazzolo Acreide, the Natale and Di Nuovo caves at Termini Imerese, that of Cala dei Genovesi in the island of Levanzo, etc., contain an industry of normal-sized implements amongst which the smallest ones (microliths) are rare or altogether absent. On the other hand, some of the other stations, such as the caves of San Teodoro, Mangiapane and others, produce large numbers of microlithic implements, frequently geometric in shape.

Often associated with this microlithic industry is a particular type of burin, known as the microburin, a type characteristic in central and western Europe of the Tardenoisian culture. In the Addaura cave, near Palermo, there were indications suggesting that this prevailingly microlithic industry with microburins was limited to the upper levels of the deposit, while it seems to have been absent from the lower strata belonging to the culture.

The shelter of Castello at Termini Imerese might be put at the end of this evolution. It is characterized by a conspicuously microlithic industry with a large number of forms amongst which there occur both geometric types (crescents and triangles) and microburins, though neither predominates.

Such a decisively microlithic tendency, and the frequent occurrence of microburins, which in Europe are characteristic of the Mesolithic period, seems to indicate that these stations belong to a final phase of the Upper Palaeolithic, or they may possibly be regarded as mesolithic.

Until the last few years nothing was known about the human

beings who lived in the palaeolithic caves in Sicily. Recently, however, the discovery of five burials in the San Teodoro cave has thrown some light on this question. Although they had been partially destroyed by wanton digging, these tombs are nevertheless of the greatest interest, since they are the only Upper Palaeolithic tombs so far discovered in Italy, with the exception of those in Liguria at Balzi Rossi and Arene Candide. The skeletons were laid on their backs with no constant orientation, and seem to have had their outstretched arms by their sides, except a very damaged one which had the fingers of the left hand close to the skull. In one of these tombs several pendants made by boring through the canine teeth of deer were dis-covered. These must certainly have formed a necklace or some other ornament. Near another tomb there were some little pebbles, and part of a deer-antler. Over the tombs a uniform layer of powdered ochre had been spread.

In the last few years an enormous interest in the Sicilian Palaeolithic has been aroused by the discovery of a notable series of works of art which we may well regard as being among the finest manifestations of palaeolithic art. The importance of these discoveries is all the greater since no other examples of quaternary art are known from Italy with the exception of the poor and schematic animal figures in the Romanelli cave in Terra d'Otranto.

The first discovery was made in 1950 in a small cave at Cala dei Genovesi on the island of Levanzo, one of the Egadi group. This little island, like Favignana, near by, must, during the marine regressions of the Pleistocene, have been joined to Sicily, from which it is separated today only by shallow water. In one interior room of the cave two distinct series of figures were discovered, one series incised, and the other painted.

Fig. 1   Painted pebbles from the Grotta della Cala dei Genovesi in Levanzo. Heights 2¾" and 3⅛"

The incised figures, mostly representing animals, are viva-ciously naturalistic. They depict red deer, oxen (*Bos primigenius*) and equids, which, to judge from the big head set on a slender neck and from the short ears and weak legs, must certainly represent the *hydruntinus*.

Particularly lively is the figure of a young doe, turning its head, surely one of the most beautiful expressions of quaternary art in Sicily.

Plate 1

The figures are traced in simple profile, but with a sure touch and with a vivid sense of reality. Very occasionally some particular anatomical feature, such as the eye, is indicated. With these figures we must also connect the figure of a bovid, drawn not on the walls of the cave but on a loose stone.

The painted figures, on the other hand, are represented schematically; they are stiff and far removed from the naturalness of the incised drawings. They are anthropomorphic figures, in which one can distinguish a progressive schematization leading to forms which no longer bear any similarity to the human body; like the little pottery idols of the Mediterranean Neolithic and Bronze Ages, with shapes like violins or bottles which degenerate to cylinders and crosses. More rarely there are little figures of quadrupeds or of fishes, which are rather more true to nature.

Plate 2

Although so different from each other in their artistic conception, a certain link between the two series is shown in a group of three human figures, one of which is bearded, and apparently dancing. These are all incised, but in a less realistic style than that of the animal figures done in the same technique. Comparable with these is a small figure painted in red (instead of in black like the others), much more naturalistic and in some details closely akin to one of the incised human figures.

Fig. 2

Plate 3

Considering the fact that there are Gravettian levels in the external chamber of the cave, and that the artistic style of the incised figures is like Upper Palaeolithic art in other regions, there can be little doubt that they belong to that period. But the dating of the painted figures is more difficult. P. Graziosi, to whom we owe the publication of this cave, links these painted figures with the schematic rock-paintings of Spain, and with the small earthenware idols commonly found in the Bronze Age in Crete, the Cyclades and at Troy. There are in

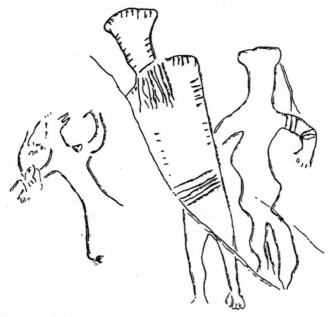

Fig. 2   Incised anthropomorphic figures from the Grotta della Cala dei Genovesi in the island of Levanzo. Height of taller figure 12".

fact traces of sporadic occupation in post-Palaeolithic times in the Levanzo cave.

One is uncertain how to date the two pebbles, decorated with groups of lines painted with red ochre, dug up in a strip of disturbed soil in the same cave. These show a vague affinity with the well-known ones from Mas d'Azil, as well as to those from the Azilian levels of Arene Candide, and to those from the Grotta delle Felci in Capri, but here again they are of uncertain date.

Fig. 1

31

The discovery of the paintings and *graffiti* in the Levanzo cave was followed soon afterwards by an important discovery made by Signora I. Marconi Bovio of a series of incised draw, ings in one of the Addaura caves on the northern side of Monte Pellegrino in the outskirts of Palermo.

The particular interest of the Addaura discovery lies in the fact that this time we have not only figures of animals such as are usually depicted in quaternary art, but human figures as well, sometimes isolated and sometimes arranged in a composed group. Signora Marconi Bovio distinguished three groups of figures differing from each other both in style and technique. Sometimes they partly overlap each other, and so provide a hint as to the relative date of the groups.

The first group includes figures generally drawn with a light thin line, with no visible connexions in the composition; amongst these are some beautiful animal figures, including a mare followed by her colt, a young running deer, and other equids or bovids. But there are also various human figures, including a woman with pronounced belly and flabby breasts carrying a heavy bundle, and two men in lively action close by. One of these men is wearing a bird-beak mask similar to those of several figures in the second group.

Plates 4, 5

In contrast to the figures of the first group, those in the second group are incised with a much deeper line and form a complex and composed scene, with ten male figures, some of whom seem to be dancing in a ring round two re, cumbent figures, while others seem to be looking on at the scene, and another is striding towards them carrying a long spear.

Plate 4

Plate 5

Some of the dancers are raising their arms in gestures still common in modern folk dances, and others are dancing dif, ferent steps, while one with bent legs is stretching his arms forward and looking behind him. Below these and near to them is a large fallow deer which seems to be climbing up a

Plate 5

steep slope, and although this is drawn in the same deeply incised technique, its connexion with the dancers in the composition is not clear.

The human figures are drawn with the same naturalistic liveliness as are the animals, with a sure and decisive line, and acute observation of reality. Though mostly stark naked, a few of them have around their waists a thin line suggesting a belt. The hands are never shown, and the feet only rarely so. In contrast to the naturalistic treatment of the bodies is the strange way in which the faces appear to be covered by bird-beak masks. A thick mass of hair seems to frame the faces, the features of which are never indicated.

Heated discussions have taken place over the interpretation of the recumbent figures in the middle. Though these were drawn one above the other, the artist probably intended us to imagine them lying beside each other. They face in opposite directions, in similar attitudes. One leans on his forearm, the other on his elbows, and both have their chests upright. The first at least is in an unnatural position, violently constricted, with his legs forcibly bent, so that his feet are near his buttocks, and although less clearly drawn, the second figure may probably have been in a similar position.

A. C. Blanc and Ginetta Chiappella have recently suggested that these drawings represent a scene of torture or sacrifice, or rather a hanging effected by forcibly tying the feet to the neck, and they interpret the ithyphallic appearance of the figures as the result of strangulation. But Signora Marconi Bovio does not accept this hypothesis. It is probable, however, that this shows us a scene of initiation or of a propitiatory rite, with some hint of sexual practices connected with the idea of perpetuating the tribe.

The third group among the Addaura figures is represented only by two isolated figures of bovids, drawn with a hard angular outline, in a style neither lively nor naturalistic. Stiffly

Fig. 3

33

drawn, they suggest a decadence from the artistic level of the earlier drawings.

A third outstanding group of incised figures has recently been discovered by Signora Marconi Bovio in another cave, the Niscemi cave on the east side of Monte Pellegrino facing the Parco della Favorita. Here are animal figures only, and they are incised in a style very closely resembling the Levanzo drawings. The main group consists of three bovine figures with heavy, massive bodies on very short legs, and two wild horses (*hydruntinus?*), some features of which, like the eye and the brushlike mane, are drawn in an unusual way. Another figure standing by itself is a young male deer.

When Raymond Vaufrey outlined the first synthesis of the Palaeolithic in Italy in 1928, he regarded Sicily, from the standpoint of prehistoric archaeology, as being *au bout du monde*. But now, the discovery of the engravings at Levanzo and Addaura and in the Niscemi cave raises it to a position of the first magnitude in the panorama of the European Palaeolithic. These discoveries also pose a number of questions concerning the possible connexions between these drawings and others in more distant regions, but at present it is premature to try to find the answers.

2. THE MESOLITHIC

In Sicily it is more difficult than in other places to make a sharp distinction between the Upper Palaeolithic and the Mesolithic, i.e. between the cultures which flourished during the last Glacial period and those at the beginning of the Holocene, when the Würmian glaciation was over and the climate was becoming stabilized into the conditions of the present day.

There are two considerations which render such a distinction difficult. On the one hand, there is the fact that, owing to its southern latitude, Sicily never had a glacial climate, but had a phase of more intense precipitation instead (like the pluvial periods in Africa), to which the numerous dry valleys (like

Fig. 3   Incised schematized bovid from the Addaura cave. Length 17".

African 'wadis') in the limestone regions of south-eastern Sicily bear witness.

The Sicilian Pleistocene fauna of the Glacial period follow-ing after the warm fauna with pachyderms is, as we have already mentioned, not very specialized and lacks elements specifically connected with a cold climate. It does not seem, therefore, to have undergone substantial changes caused by the climatic variations marking the end of the Glacial period, i.e. the transition from the Pleistocene to the Holocene.

On the other hand, as far as is known today, it seems that Sicily never had those cultures, so well defined in character, which represent the Mesolithic on the European continent. The Sicilian stations, which we should incline to regard as meso‑lithic, seem actually, from a typological standpoint, to show a very long lingering persistence of Upper Palaeolithic forms, even though they contain some new industrial types.

We have seen in the preceding chapter how the Upper Palaeolithic of the Gravettian type in Sicily seems to have evolved towards forms more and more markedly microlithic. But they still retained the same fundamental characteristics. We have already described how this accentuated use of microliths, as well as the presence of 'microburins' (which by now were characteristic of the mesolithic cultures in Europe), indicate a later date for the stations in a more advanced stage of this evolution, and above all for the rock‑shelter of Castello at Termini Imerese, which seems to represent its termination.

Perhaps only two stations in Sicily represent the real and proper Mesolithic: the Corruggi cave at Pachino and the rock‑shelter of Sperlinga at San Basilio near Novara di Sicilia. In both we witness the same phenomenon. The cultural layer (overlying the clay of the caves, which is barren of human industry) is characterized by a stone industry of strongly micro‑lithic character, which in the lower levels is found alone, but in the upper levels is associated with pottery and obsidian. This pottery is of Stentinello type, the earliest neolithic pottery in Sicily.

At the Corruggi cave, where this fact was observed for the first time, one was inclined to think that this association did not indicate true contemporaneity, but rather that it was a casual mixture brought about at a period still very early, but later than the filling of the cave. This possibility must be excluded in the case of Sperlinga, where, in the higher levels, in which pottery is associated with a microlithic industry, there are found some tiny implements identical with the flint ones, but made of obsidian imported from the near‑by island of Lipari.

Both the Corruggi and Sperlinga caves would show, then, the existence in Sicily of nuclei of mesolithic peoples who at a certain period came into contact with the first neolithic peoples who had settled in the island: with the bearers, that is to say, of the Stentinello civilization, from whom they would have received both pottery and obsidian. Even so, these mesolithic peoples must have survived for some time, keeping their own traditions, and especially the stone industry of Tardenoisian type which differs radically from that of the Stentinello villages. But in the Corruggi cave and Sperlinga the absolute identity between the industries from the strata without pottery and those with the earliest pottery and obsidian, shows that even the former strata cannot date back to a very ancient time, but must only slightly antedate the Neolithic. As a matter of fact, although the stone industry of these stations retains many of the features of the Upper Palaeolithic in Sicily, it also provides new elements, particularly in the increased tendency towards geometric microliths.

We find now a greater number of triangles and crescents, and, perhaps for the first time, trapezes and lozenge-shaped implements, while microburins, even if rare, are always present. The great number of back-blades and points of different sizes, of wavy-edged blades, punches, end-scrapers, and of polyhedral *bec de flûte*, and side burins, corresponds to what we have seen in the Sicilian Upper Palaeolithic stations, while the presence of small discoidal scrapers reminds us of Castello at Termini Imerese.

The fauna of the Corruggi cave does not really differ from that of the Upper Palaeolithic stations, and among the food refuse there are still found a lot of remains of *Equus* (*Asinus*) *hydruntinus*, which therefore seems to have survived right up to the dawn of the Neolithic.

Chapter II

The Neolithic

1. THE STENTINELLO CULTURE

THE EARLIEST NEOLITHIC CULTURE so far known in Sicily is that of Stentinello, so called after the village of that name near Syracuse where it was first recognized by Orsi in 1890. Certainly this culture cannot be regarded as a development from the palaeolithic or mesolithic which preceded it in Sicily, and with which it seems to have nothing in common. In particular, it does not carry on the palaeolithic and mesolithic tradition in flint working.

According to our present stage of knowledge the arrival of the Stentinello culture seems to have been a novel event which suddenly interrupted the slow evolution of the palaeolithic and mesolithic which had lasted for thousands of years, and brought them to an abrupt end.

Without any doubt the advent of the Neolithic in Sicily was associated with the landing of new peoples on the coast of the island: peoples coming from distant shores, bringing with them a civilization by far superior to that of the peoples who had lived in Sicily up to now. These newly arrived peoples no longer depended on hunting and the collection of wild fruits for their sustenance, but knew how to produce their own food. They understood by now how to farm, and to breed and rear animals. They crossed the seas with their small boats, and even traded with far-off peoples, exchanging with them their products and learning from them new ideas and techniques.

They no longer lived in caves, but built themselves huts clustered in villages which were often fortified. They made pottery in which they displayed their artistic sense. As well as flint, they now used the sharper obsidian and made axes by

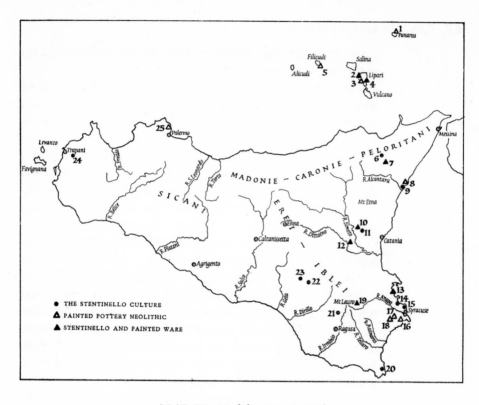

MAP III   Neolithic Sites in Sicily

1	Calcara	14	Stentinello
2	Castellaro	15	Grotte di Siracusa
3	Piano Conte	16	Matrensa
4	Lipari acropolis	17	Grotta del Conzo
5	Capo Graziano	18	Grotta Chiusazza
6	Abacaenum	19	Grotta Masella
7	San Basilio	20	Grotta Corruggi
8	Taormina	21	Calaforno
9	Naxos	22	S. Ippolito
10	Paternò—Trefontane	23	Monte Scala
11	Fontana di Pepe	24	Paceco
12	Poggio Rosso	25	Monte Pellegrino
13	Megara Hyblaea	26	Termini Imerese

polishing basalt and greenstone. They did not yet know the use of the bow and arrow, but probably used slings.

The advent of the Stentinello culture in Sicily was no isolated fact. We can affirm, on the contrary, that it was only one episode in a far wider historical process: the spread of the Neolithic over the whole of the Mediterranean.

On all the shores of the Mediterranean the earliest neolithic cultures seem closely akin to one another. They are all in fact characterized by rough pottery coarsely decorated by impressions or incisions made in the soft clay before baking. The patterns are often made with the edge of shells, and the fact that they are almost everywhere identical demonstrates the fundamental unity of these cultures.

The Stentinello pottery fits perfectly, both technically and stylistically, into this wider complex of impressed pottery, and it is perhaps one of its most artistically advanced developments. In fact, this impressed pottery characterizes the earliest neolithic levels so far brought to light in northern Syria (Ugarit, Judeideh, Byblos, Chagar Bazar, Arpachiyah, etc.), and in the south of Anatolia (Sakçe Gözü and Mersin). Hints of it are found, too, in the Balkan peninsula (pre-Sesklo culture on the Greek mainland, Starčevo culture, etc.).

The same types of pottery characterize the earliest Neolithic in Apulia and Abruzzi (Molfetta culture), the lowest neolithic levels in the caves of Liguria (Arene Candide) and southern France (Fontbrégua, Châteauneuf-les-Martigues, caves of the Gardon valley).

Identical pottery decoration is typical of the earliest neolithic culture in Catalonia (Monserrat) and in eastern Spain (Cueva de la Sarsa, etc.). We also find the same kind of pottery all along the North African coast, at Tangiers (Achakar), in Algeria (caves and snail-middens of the Oran district), in Tunisia (Redeyef), in Libya (Fezzan) and in the Sudan. The coastal distribution of these earlier neolithic Mediterranean cultures with impressed pottery, as well as their presence in small islands (Levkas, Corfù, Tremiti, Malta, Lipari, Elba, Corsica), witnesses to a diffusion by sea perhaps from some centre which today we are inclined to look for in the Near East, for this appears to us more and more to have been the source of neolithic civilization.

We are led to surmise that the people who migrated across the Mediterranean, bringing the earliest agriculture to the coasts of the Balkans, Italy, France, Spain and North Africa, came from the coastal regions of northern Syria and southern Anatolia—regions where this type of culture is not only in evidence, but also far richer and more widespread than any-where else.

Although our knowledge of the subject is so far very limited, there is ground for supposing that the diffusion of the Early Neolithic with impressed pottery in the Mediterranean is itself only an episode in a process affecting the whole of the ancient world.

Impressed pottery, closely akin to that of the Mediterranean, also characterizes the earliest known neolithic cultures from China to South Africa and the Gulf of Guinea. The very immensity of the territory affected by this process is a witness to its long duration.

But to confine our inquiry to the Mediterranean itself; can we get any idea of the date when the first wave of neolithic culture spread over it? We think that this date can be estab-lished, even if somewhat approximately.

In the Near East, in Syria and in the south of Anatolia, this earliest neolithic impressed pottery was at some time super-seded by painted pottery of a far higher artistic and technical standard, due to the advent of new, more evolved cultures —those of Samarra and Tel Halaf.

Although it is as yet very difficult to assess the exact date of this transition, we do not believe we are far wrong in thinking that it occurred not later than the beginning of the fourth millennium B.C.

And so, if the diffusion of the neolithic impressed pottery over the Mediterranean really started from the Anatolian and Syrian shores, and if it really was brought by sea (which, if true, seems to exclude the possibility of prolonged stops in its progress), it is obvious that it must have happened before the supposed mother-culture had been replaced in the Near East by fresh painted pottery cultures, i.e. not later than the end of the fifth or the beginning of the fourth millennium B.C.

Hitherto the Stentinello culture is chiefly known on the east coast of Sicily, perhaps because that is the best explored part of the island. We have already mentioned traces of it in the Corruggi cave at Pachino. Near Syracuse three fortified villages, Stentinello and Megara Hyblaea to the north, and Matrensa to the south of the town, have been discovered. The first two of these were surrounded by a continuous ditch cut in the soft limestone and backed by a stone rampart. At Matrensa it seems that the ditch was discontinuous. We have traces of the same culture from the Caltagirone district in the villages of Sant' Ippolito and Monte Scala. The only grave belonging to this culture so far known was found in the fee of Calaforno near Monterosso Almo. It was an oval grave, surrounded and paved with slabs of stone. Another important series of finds came from the neighbourhood of Paternò on the southern slopes of Etna, excavated by Corrado Cafici: the villages of Trefontane, Poggio Rosso and Fontana di Pepe.

Signs of the same culture have also been recognized from farther north in the province of Messina: at Naxos, in a small cave near Capo di Taormina, on a site near to the ancient Abacaenum, and in the rock-shelter of Sperlinga at San Basilio. Lately a Stentinello site has been discovered at Castellaro Vecchio in the island of Lipari. Discoveries of pottery in the Stentinello style from the Geraci cave at Termini Imerese and from Paceco near Trapani show that this civilization also extended into western Sicily. Moreover, similar pottery is also found in Malta, at Ghar Dalam (Dalam cave) and elsewhere. As we have said, the pottery characteristic of Stentinello is

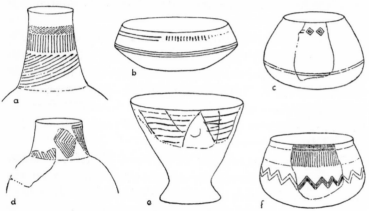

Fig. 4   Pottery of the Stentinello culture:
(a–d) *from Stentinello;*
(e, f) *from Matrensa. Height of* (e) *approx.* 12½", *others to scale.*

decorated with impressions or incisions made in the soft clay before it was baked. The two classes into which this pottery can be divided are always found in close association and are apparently strictly contemporaneous. The first class consists of coarser ware, in which open forms (i.e. those with their biggest diameter at the mouth) predominate; these include bowls, cups and fruit dishes on high stands. The very rough decoration was frequently made with the finger-nail or with various punches, sometimes even with the edge of *Cardium* or *Pectunculus* shells. At other times it consisted of hatched triangles.

Fig. 4, e

The second class of pottery is made of finer ware, smoother and more polished, and this time the prevalent forms are closed, i.e. with the mouth somewhat narrower than the body of the pot, and they always have a convex base.

Fig. 4

Plates 6–9

The decorations are emphasized by white chalky incrustation, and are often very exuberant, covering the entire surface of the pot. But there are other vases with a much more sober ornament, limited to one or two narrow lines of decoration, or to a slight band round the rim, and there are many undecorated vases as well.

At Stentinello, Matrensa and Megara Hyblaea this line is often interrupted by two lozenges representing stylized human eyes. This prophylactic eyemotif is more evident in the Etna sites, where the eyelashes are also shown. At Trefontane we find a little vase with a human face. At Stentinello there are also some specimens of clay animals, and some little earthenware idols.

Fig. 4, c

Plates 11–13
Plate 14
Plate 10

The flint industry includes, in the main, big regular blades, not as a rule retouched, but occasionally retouched on the flaked surface, or made into points or endscrapers. Obsidian, imported from Lipari, is also common, and there are basalt axes, querns and grainrubbers made of lava; at Matrensa there were also some slingstones. Bone implements are rare, and they include some points and spatulae.

In some of the sites of this civilization (Stentinello, Trefontane, Taormina, Lipari, and especially Megara Hyblaea) pottery is occasionally found which is made of finer paste, painted with red bands or flames on a light background. Owing to its rarity, this painted ware may be regarded as an import.

Plate 15

Identical pottery is found in southern Italy, in the Apulian caves, and in the fortified villages of the Matera district; these are actually very similar to those of Stentinello and Megara Hyblaea. In southern Italy, however, this painted pottery appears to be absent in the earlier stage of the Neolithic, when pottery decorated with impressions made before firing seems to be exclusive. In fact, it only seems to appear in the second stage, when the impressed ware is still being made, but by now associated with new cultural elements.

The Stentinello culture, as we know it from the villages in the Syracuse and Etna districts, shows indeed considerably more evolved features than the other Mediterranean cultures with impressed pottery, and possesses elements absent in the earliest neolithic groups, and which, at least in the eastern Mediterranean, seem to characterize the more advanced cultural stages. These include the fortified villages, the painted pottery, the varied forms of impressed pottery and the complexity of its decoration, and the little earthenware idols and animals. So that, although the Stentinello culture blossomed on the main stem of the Mediterranean impressed pottery cultures, it seems to have been a late development, and to have been contem-poraneous with the first diffusion of painted ware in southern Italy.

So far no indications of an earlier and less developed stage of the Stentinello culture has been found, and as we know it, it always appears to be fully evolved.

The reason for this apparent delay in the diffusion of the Neolithic in Sicily can perhaps be guessed at, even if not demonstrated with certainty, when one tries to trace the routes by which it may have spread from east to west. Its diffusion, as we have said before, was probably effected by sea. But know-ledge of navigation was at this time in its infancy, and probably the crossing of wide expanses of sea was impossible. It was, rather, a coastal navigation linking one island to another one visible in the same archipelago.

It seems clear, however, that the Adriatic was traversed, be it directly across the Otranto channel or, more probably, by way of the islands of Pelagosa, Pianosa, Tremiti and the Gargano peninsula; this may explain the presence of this culture at Tremiti, and its wide diffusion along the whole coast of Apulia.

Its expansion must have followed not only the Adriatic coast northwards as far as the Marche, but also the Ionic coast to the south-west, and developed all over the rich coastal plain from Taranto to Sibari, which then was not yet malaria-infested. The rocky countryside of Calabria which begins at this point, and which has scanty water and few plains, must have been an obstacle rather than an attraction to these peoples; so the further expansion of neolithic culture must have been carried out instead through the Apennine passes towards the Tyrrhenian Sea, and along its coasts, reaching northwards to Elba and the Ligurian coast, and westwards to Provence and Spain. Calabria and Sicily must have remained outside this first colonizing movement (just as later they were excluded from the earliest Greek colonization which reached the Campanian coasts instead), and must only later have moved into the orbit of the new neolithic civilization, at the time when the Middle Neolithic painted pottery was just beginning to replace the Early Neolithic impressed ware in Italy.

2. THE NEOLITHIC PAINTED-POTTERY CULTURES

While the first wave of neolithic culture to sweep over the Mediterranean was characterized by impressed pottery, the succeeding wave was characterized by painted pottery.

Here again we are dealing with a historical phenomenon of the widest range, probably affecting the whole of Asia as well. In China, in fact, as well as on the shores of the Mediterranean, the earliest neolithic levels with impressed ware are overlaid by those with painted pottery of a higher artistic standard, which technically, and often stylistically, is in its decoration closely comparable to the pottery of the Near East.

Links between these widely separated regions have now been found in the cultures of Central Asia, India and Iran. It is likely that Mesopotamia began its cultural development at this point.

We have already mentioned the Samarra and Tel Halaf cultures which, probably at the end of the fifth or early in the fourth millennium B.C., spread over northern Syria and into southern Anatolia, bringing to an end those cultures with impressed pottery that had preceded them. But the painted-pottery cultures not only reached the Mediterranean from Mesopotamia and Syria: another branch, pushing across South Russia, Rumania and Bulgaria, reached the Greek mainland, while from the Balkans they spread to southern Italy by way of the Otranto channel, and found the most westerly point of their expansion in Sicily and the Aeolian Islands.

The neolithic painted-pottery cultures are far more evolved than those with impressed pottery, and the cultural elements which they possess are much more numerous. Their pottery, both in shape and in decoration, often attains a very high standard of design and artistic taste, and some hint of their religious cults is supplied by numerous little earthenware idols. In this civilization, copper smelting was known in the East from a very early stage, even if not from its remotest origins.

In the mainland of Greece, which concerns us most closely because of its proximity to southern Italy, it has been possible to define three clear stages in the basic evolution of the painted-pottery culture. The first (Sesklo period) is characterized by a two-colour decoration, and spiral and meander motifs are un-known. The second (Dimini period) has a three-colour ware, making frequent use of spiral and meander motifs, and the third (Rachmani period) is characterized by encrusted (white on dark) ware, and by pottery with burnished decoration.

The close connexion between the neolithic painted wares of southern Italy facing the Adriatic (Apulia, the Matera district and the Abruzzi), and those of the Greek mainland, has always been evident, but a total lack of systematic excavation in these regions has made it impossible to establish their stylistic and chronological evolution on a stratigraphic basis. A useful attempt to overcome this difficulty, even if without the support of stratigraphy, has recently been made by R. B. K. Stevenson. But only in the last few years has it been possible to outline it very clearly as a result of the excavations on the island of Lipari, where the levels belonging to this age are extraordinarily rich, and overlie each other with extreme regularity.

We will therefore begin by examining the remains of this period in the Aeolian Islands.

3. THE NEOLITHIC CIVILIZATIONS IN THE AEOLIAN ISLANDS

The Aeolian Islands enjoyed a flourishing civilization during the Neolithic period. Their prosperity was due to the exploitation of obsidian, a volcanic glass, erupted from the craters of Forgia Vecchia and of Monte Pelato in the island of Lipari.

Obsidian is sharper than flint, even if less easily worked, and it was a product much in demand before metal techniques were developed. Worked in the villages and huts scattered everywhere in the Aeolian Islands, and struck into irregular and very sharp flakes, obsidian was widely traded not only over all Sicily and South Italy, but probably also to much more distant parts of the central and western Mediterranean. The enormous quantities of cores and of waste flakes which are recovered from the neolithic villages in the Aeolian Islands, and which are scattered about everywhere in the fields, reflect the intensity of this industry, which must have lasted for centuries, assuring the inhabitants of a standard of living certainly higher than that of many other nearby regions, including Sicily itself.

The exploitation of obsidian in Lipari must have begun very early if it was already found so abundantly in the villages of the Stentinello culture in Sicily, and in the earliest pottery levels of Sperlinga at San Basilio.

The earliest of the villages so far discovered in the Aeolian Islands, that of Castellaro Vecchio, near Quattropani, in the island of Lipari, belongs to the Stentinello culture; it had both the characteristic impressed pottery and pottery painted with unbordered red bands.

The position in which this upland village is situated, in one of the most fertile parts of the island, is more favourable for tilling and the pasturing of animals than for navigation and the trading of obsidian, and perhaps shows that these earliest settlers in the islands held strongly to the agricultural and pastoral traditions and to the economic organization of their previous habitat. But the enormous quantity of obsidian chips which may be found there indicates that the working of this mineral now constituted the main activity of the village.

Castellaro Vecchio is so far the only village of its kind which has been identified in the islands, but was surely not the only one originally, and it is probable that others of the same period remain to be discovered.

So far no evidence of this period has been found on the Lipari acropolis, though in all the succeeding periods right up to the present day this was chosen for the most important settlement within the Aeolian archipelago.

The Castello of Lipari is an isolated mass of rhyolite which rises precipitously from the sea, forming two small harbours— Marina Lunga on the north and Marina Corta on the south. It is a natural fortress and was certainly chosen for that reason by the Neolithic and Bronze Age people for their settlement, and later for the acropolis of the Greek, Roman and medieval towns.

The traces of the different civilizations which succeeded each other here form superimposed layers regularly stratified for a depth of about thirty feet. Here, in fact, we have a real 'tell' like those of the Near East.

Settlement on the Castello seems to have been established at a time immediately succeeding that of Castellaro Vecchio. The earliest strata which have been found, and which rest directly on the live rock, show in fact a neolithic culture characterized by the wide diffusion of a painted pottery, differing from that of Castellaro Vecchio and the Materan villages by having the bands and red 'flames', which always form the fundamental

Plates 16, 17   motif of the decoration, outlined by a black border. The forms of the pots also seem to be different. Since this style was first noticed in the Grotta delle Felci in the island of Capri, it has come to be known as the 'Capri' style. Pottery of the Stentinello kind, decorated with impressions made before firing, had almost completely disappeared by this time, and is represented only by a few varied fragments. In its place now there is plenty of pottery made of black or brown paste, very smooth and

Fig. 5   polished, perfectly made and almost always plain; only occa-sionally it has a restrained scratched decoration, or is painted in red ochre on the dark background after firing. These decora-

Fig. 5, a   tions seem to be almost exclusively on spherical pots with large mouths and low vertical rims. In a third class of pottery, a tempered ware with incised decoration, we find spiral-meander decoration for the first time. The head of a little earthenware idol also came from these levels.

In an extremely rich stone industry the staple material is almost always obsidian; flint is very rarely found, as it has to be imported, and was used only for making very carefully worked implements.

The succeeding layers, representing the third period of the Aeolian Neolithic, are characterized by pottery painted with motifs which are generally complicated derivatives from the spiral and meander. Another very common motif is the bordered zigzag. The forms of the pots are now much more sophisticated than those of the preceding periods. The handles are unusual, and are made with a clay strip coiled into complicated patterns.

The same motifs that were used in the painted decorations sometimes recur in a few clay seals or *pintaderas*.

This decorative style has been called the 'Serra d'Alto' style, after the village in the Matera district where it is best represented.

The following period, the fourth in the Aeolian Neolithic,

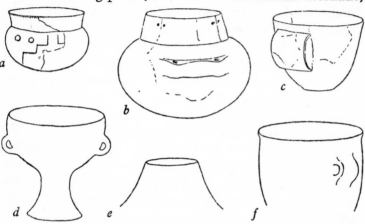

Fig. 5   *Forms of brown ware belonging to the second phase of the Aeolian Neolithic, from the lower levels of the Lipari acropolis. Lipari Museum.*

shows a reaction from the excessively 'baroque' trends of the preceding periods. Painted decoration is no longer used, and is replaced by a monochrome red pottery, with much simpler shapes and lugs which are generally tubular or spool-shaped. Slag from copper smelting shows that metal-working techniques were already known.

Fig. 6

The layers of this period in the Lipari acropolis are somewhat thin. The chief settlement is now no longer on the acropolis itself, but below it in the rich Diana plain, on the western edge of the modern town, and we may therefore call the pottery style of this period the 'Diana' style.

The excavation of the extremely rich Diana site has revealed a great wealth of pottery and stone objects, which has enabled us to recognize at least three distinct stages in this cultural phase.

In the first stage the shapes of the pots are still very similar to those of the 'Serra d'Alto' style, and still retain the high rims, though by now the characteristic handles are spool-shaped or cylindrical.

In the following stage the rims are far lower; the spool-shaped handles are longer and more slender, but the surface of the pottery is still the same fine coral-red colour.

In the final stages of the Diana culture rims are practically abolished, and the handles are either reduced to a mere symbol without any functional value, or are sometimes heavier, and widely splayed at their ends. There is a degeneration in the quality of the glaze, which loses the fine red colour of the earlier stages, and is brownish or purplish instead.

Fig. 6, d, f

At Piano Conte on the Lipari plain a smaller village has recently been discovered which belongs exclusively to this last stage. The Diana culture is also found at the Calcara site in the island of Panarea and at Capo Graziano in the island of Filicudi.

4. THE NEOLITHIC PAINTED-POTTERY CULTURES IN SICILY AND SOUTH ITALY

So far, in Sicily, there are very few indications of the several styles of pottery decoration whose sequence is so clearly known from Lipari. Without this stratigraphy we should not have had enough evidence to show us the various stages in the pottery evolution. It is possible that during the time when the pottery painted with black-bordered red stripes or 'flames' in the Capri style was flourishing in the Aeolian Islands, the Stentinello culture was still lingering on in Sicily, preserving all the elements which had characterized it in the preceding stage. But there is no definite evidence for this: only a hint from the fact that amongst the painted sherds found at Megara Hyblaea and

Trefontane, associated with pottery decorated with unbordered red stripes, there were plenty of sherds of three-colour ware decorated with bordered, red stripes.

Plate 15

The spiral-meander style is known from one small vase found on Monte Pellegrino near Palermo, and from some

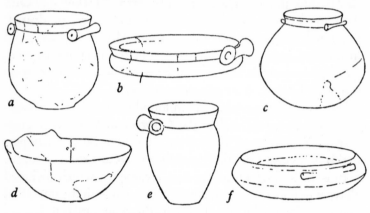

Fig. 6   Characteristic forms of monochrome red ware of the Late Neolithic:
  (a) *from Matrensa;*
  (b) *from Megara Hyblaea;*
  (c) *from Marmo di Paternò;*
  (d *and* f) *from the Diana site in Lipari;*
  (e) *from Paternò. Height of* (e) *approx.* $5\frac{1}{2}''$, *others to scale.*
    Syracuse Museum (a, c, e); *Lipari Museum* (d, f).

found near Paternò. Two of these have very complicated scroll-handles, perhaps the richest and most complicated examples known of the type.

Plate 20

Two more from the neighbourhood of Paternò seem to belong to the transitional phase between the spiral-meander style and the Diana style. The handles by this time are of the tubular or spool type, and the painted decoration is extremely restrained; it is reduced to only a few strokes of bordered zigzag. These pots may be contemporaneous with the somewhat similar ones from the huts in the Gravela fee of Serra d'Alto, near Matera, and themselves the ultimate products of the style of this period.

In the following period in Sicily, characterized by mono-chrome red pottery of the Diana style, examples are much more numerous. Pots of this type have been found at Sperlinga di San Basilio; in a few places around Paternò (Trefontane, Orto del Conte, tombs in the Marmo fee); in the Syracuse district, in a tomb discovered near the village of Megara Hyblaea, and in another near that of Matrensa, but the relations between these tombs and the villages near by is unknown, as there is no similarity between their respective pottery.

Fig. 6

Signs of this pottery have been found recently in the Masella cave near Buscemi, and in the Conzo and Chiusazza caves between Syracuse and Canicattini. In central Sicily a few pots in this style come from the Vecchiuzzo cave at Petralia Sottana.

In none of these places (except Trefontane, which included all types of pottery) is the red ware associated with the impressed pottery of Stentinello type. In Sicily, therefore, just as in Lipari, the red, Diana style ware seems to be characteristic of a well-defined cultural phase in the Late Neolithic, when the impressed Stentinello pottery had already disappeared.

It is an interesting fact that sherds of red, Diana style pottery have been found at Mġar and Borg-in-Nadur in Malta and at Santa Verna in Gozo contemporaneous with one of the earliest stages (even if not the very beginning) of the local megalithic architecture (i.e. in the IA1 or IA2 periods of Evans's classification).

We can assume from these indications that, during the Neolithic period, the Sicilian cultural evolution was identical with, or at least very similar to, that in the Aeolian Islands known to us from the excavations on the Lipari acropolis.

In southern Italy there seem to be clear indications of an earlier Neolithic, in which impressed ware is exclusive, and which does not include any painted ware (lower levels of

Coppa Nevigata at Manfredonia, of the Guardiano cave near Polignano a Mare, sites at Gaudiano, Tremiti, etc.).

Then at a later stage the impressed pottery begins to be associated with a painted ware with unbordered red bands or 'flames', identical to that from Megara Hyblaea and with scratched ware decorated after firing, or at least after drying. This is the period to which the ditched villages of Matera type belong, and also the majority of the deposits in the Apulian caves.

In southern Italy there is a far less clear distinction than in Lipari between the stage characterized by pottery painted with unbordered stripes and that with the three-colour ware, though two main groups belonging to this period are known. The first has pottery very like that from the Lipari acropolis, and is so far known only from a few pots from the Grotta delle Felci in the island of Capri. The second, on the other hand, is widely diffused on the Italian mainland, though chiefly found in the Ripoli village near Téramo in the Abruzzi. Impressed ware is not found either at Capri or Ripoli, and, as in Lipari, it must have already disappeared by this time.

Spiral-meander ware is found widely in Apulia and in the Matera district, and where there are unmixed levels of this period, as in some of the huts at Serra d'Alto near Matera and in the Madonna di Grottole site near Polignano a Mare, no impressed pottery has been found.

The red ware of the Diana style is also widespread in southern Italy. It is known to us from the tombs of Scoglio del Tonno and Masseria Bellavista near Taranto, from Zinzulusa at Otranto, the Latronico cave, from Capri, and even as far afield as Norcia in Umbria. The cultural succession of southern Italy was even closer to that of Lipari than was the cultural succession of Sicily.

The five stylistic stages which we can recognize in the evolution of the neolithic civilization in southern Italy, the Aeolian Islands and Sicily seem to be closely related to one another. It seems possible to consider them as five successive stages in the evolution of a culture which, though changing under the influence of new ideas, and new tendencies reaching it from the East, remains fundamentally unitary. In a world in which impressed ware is almost exclusively predominant, it is not difficult to observe the first tentative introduction of painted pottery with unbordered red stripes on a light background. We can follow the gradual spread of this new type of pottery until it prevails over the impressed ware, which is eventually almost completely superseded. We can follow the evolution of the painted ware, which at first has two, then three colours, and is later decorated with meanders and spirals, becoming richer and heavier, while the handles grow more and more complicated.

We form the impression that at a certain time these somewhat 'baroque' shapes were no longer pleasing to these people, whose taste inclined towards simpler forms.

The handles become schematic, the painted decoration gets more and more sober until it disappears altogether, to be replaced by a monochrome, glossy, red ware which at first still retains the forms of the painted ware, but later grows stiffer, showing a gradual decadence both in technique and artistic quality.

If, as we think, the pottery evolution reflects that of the society responsible for it, we should say that the neolithic world which, in southern Italy, the Aeolian Islands and in Sicily had attained a very high degree of refinement and artistry, must, after a most luxuriant flowering, have shown signs of decadence before it finally disappeared.

Without any doubt the inspiration behind each of the stages in this evolution came from the Aegean and the Balkans, or at least reached Italy from that direction. The parallel develop-ment of this evolution in Greece and Italy is enough to demonstrate this.

The painted pottery with two-colour stripes obviously corre-sponds to the Sesklo period on the Greek mainland. The spiral-meander ware of the Serra d'Alto style should equate with that from Dimini, even if its very complicated handles seem to represent a strictly local specialization. The intermediate stage, that of three-colour ware with black-edged bands (not yet including spiral-meanders) of Capri and Ripoli type, does not seem to have an equivalent stage in Greece.

But the three-colour decoration does not appear in Thessaly before the beginning of the Dimini stage, so we cannot regard these Italian wares as being earlier. This would explain the presence of the spiral-meander decoration in the contemporary 'tempered' ware.

The painted ware would then have been late in taking on the spiral-meander decoration which was already widespread in other classes of pottery, and must instead have retained traditional patterns for a long while. The age of the Italian spiral-meander painted pottery would then correspond only to the advanced stages of the Dimini culture.

It is far more difficult to recognize the cultural trends lying behind the origins of the Diana style. Perhaps we should look for them in the middle stages of Troy I, and in the corresponding levels of the 'Green' (fourth) period of Poliochni in the island of Lemnos, where one finds the same tendency to exaggerate the ends of the tubular handles or to reduce the handles to a mere symbol. But no connecting links have so far been found in the intervening lands.

If, however, such a hypothesis proved to be correct, it would be the first sign of that grandiose cultural phenomenon which was to influence the whole evolution of the following period.

5. SICILY AND THE WESTERN NEOLITHIC

For a better understanding of the position which Sicily occupied in the Mediterranean Neolithic, and of this island's contribution to it, we should do well to make a rapid survey of the regions farther to the north and west of those which we have so far discussed.

While the painted-pottery cultures were spreading over the south of Italy, the Aeolian Islands and Sicily, the north of Italy presented a completely different cultural aspect.

It was gravitating into the orbit of that complex of cultures which was developing at this time in the valleys of the Middle Danube and its chief tributaries, particularly in the Tisza river.

The cultures which are now flourishing in northern Italy, especially in Emilia (Fiorano and Chiozza cultures), and in Liguria (middle levels of Arene Candide), share many features in common with the Danubian cultures (square-mouthed vases, socketed ladles, *pintaderas*, little idols, Spondylus-shell armlets, bone buttons, etc.).

But the Danubian cultural wave never swept westwards over the Alps. Farther west, on the Mediterranean coasts of France and Spain, civilizations of an archaic type were still probably lingering on, offsprings of the first Neolithic with its impressed pottery, while the inland region lagged behind in a mesolithic economy, still not having outgrown the stage of hunting and food-gathering.

At the end of the Neolithic, probably while the red pottery of the Diana-Bellavista style was flourishing in the south, a new culture was coming into being on the coastal sweep between the mouths of the Arno and the Ebro, and this, though varying slightly from one area to another, nevertheless presented a homogeneous character over all the regions it covered. This is the culture of Sabadell, Chassey, Lagozza and Cortaillod.

Its place of origin and its process of formation and diffusion are still uncertain, but it is clear that it is not just an accident that all its characteristic forms recur in the Stentinello pottery of Sicily, and that they ultimately show a kinship with the prehistoric cultures of Egypt (Amratian).

And yet, while the Stentinello pottery shows a marked tendency towards a florid decoration, the pottery of this 'Western' civilization (Lagozza-Chassey-Cortaillod) is always undecorated. One wonders if this is not in point of fact the result of a reaction in taste away from the heavy decoration of the previous age; an analogous process to that which led from the Serra d'Alto style with its spiral-meander pattern to the red monochrome ware of the Diana style. One may go further and ask whether the two processes were not in fact closely linked; the outcome perhaps of a trend in taste and ideas, prevailing at a certain time all over the Mediterranean.

There are several indications of an approximate contem-poraneity between the Lagozza-Chassey-Cortaillod cultures and the pottery style of Diana: the association of both types of pottery in hut foundations at Norcia in Umbria (in the zone bordering the two civilizations); the presence of sherds closely similar to those of Lagozza style in the Diana levels on the Lipari acropolis; and the by now evolved character of the Lagozza-Chassey-Cortaillod culture, shown by the presence in it of spindle-whorls, rhomboid arrow-heads unknown to earlier cultures, etc. But at this stage of our knowledge only a working hypothesis is possible and further field work will, no doubt, throw light on the problem.

These Mediterranean features present in the Lagozza-Chassey-Cortaillod culture show that its initial flowering must have taken place around the shores of this sea. The distribution of the sites belonging to this culture is in fact identical with that of the preceding Early Neolithic impressed pottery culture. In Catalonia the Sabadell *facies* is mainly known from a group of oval graves with crouched skeletons (Sabadell, Solsona, etc.). In southern France and on the shores of Liguria it is, on the other hand, known almost exclusively from cave-dwellings.

And yet, compared with the impressed pottery culture, the new culture reached farther into the interior; it spread into

Lombardy and pushed up the valleys of the Rhône and its tributaries, especially those of the Saône (Camp de Chassey) and the Aar, from which it flooded over the Swiss plain (Cortaillod *facies*).

In Lombardy as well as in Switzerland, it is characterized by a curious type of dwelling, built on piles on the banks of lakes, rivers or swamps, and probably of Danubian Middle Neolithic origin.

From the Middle Neolithic cultures the Lagozza-Chassey-Cortaillod culture also inherited other elements; first amongst these was the pottery decoration scratched after firing. This fashion spread more or less widely in the coastal strip of southern France, but was found only sporadically in the Lagozza culture in Lombardy, and in the Swiss Cortaillod culture, while it is apparently unrepresented in the Sabadell culture of Catalonia.

CHAPTER III

The Copper Age

W E HAVE SEEN that the Neolithic, both in the variety of its aspects and in the evolution of the decorative style of its pottery, always represented one unit in Sicily, just as it did in the Aeolian Islands and southern Italy.

The Copper Age marked a radical change in all these regions. The change, moreover, was not confined to this area only, but can be recognized in the cultural evolution in all the lands bordering the Mediterranean. Indeed, the advent of the Copper Age represented one of the biggest social revolutions in the ancient world, and possibly an ethnical one as well.

During the Neolithic period, Sicily and the Aeolian Islands had represented the extreme western limit reached by the cultural complex characterized by painted pottery, in what can to a certain extent be regarded as the civilized world of that period. Beyond it lay a still barbarous west where a much more primitive culture lingered on, still genetically belonging to the Early Neolithic with impressed pottery.

The new wave of civilization which now swept over the Mediterranean again originated on its eastern shores, but this time it reached even the most distant western coasts, giving rise to the extremely luxuriant local cultures which were to evolve throughout the whole Bronze Age.

This time the new impetus seems to have started from Anatolia and the near-by islands, and it is in fact only here that there are found together the various cultural elements which are encountered differently associated in the derivative civiliza-tions of the western and central Mediterranean.

While the neolithic painted-pottery cultures followed their slow and apparently peaceful evolution in the southern Balkans and the Italian peninsula, a new state of affairs was maturing on the Asiatic coasts. Here cultures were developing that were cruder and less artistically refined, but were more technically advanced in the art of metal smelting. They were acquainted not only with bronze (which had made a tentative appearance in Greece by the end of the Sesklo period) but also with silver, gold and lead. This is the culture whose evolution can be followed from the excavations at Troy in the Troad, Yortan in Mysia, Poliochni in the island of Lemnos, and Thermi in Mytilene. From a still primitive culture with villages of oval huts (Poliochni I) a flourishing urban civilization quickly developed into a town surrounded by a strong wall, with broad streets and paved squares, public wells and granaries, and houses with many rooms developing round a central megaron.

The old neolithic world of painted pottery must very soon have begun to feel the impact of this new world, so much more advanced in techniques and social organization, which was reaching maturity on its borders. It may even have been due to the change in fashions and artistic sensibility brought by these Aegeo-Anatolian influences that the spiral-meander pottery was abandoned in favour of the monochrome ware of Diana-Bellavista style.

In the Copper Age, however, the intimate connexions between these Anatolian cultures and the various local ones which develop in the central and western Mediterranean are even more evident. These cultures seem to have been intimately interrelated, even though each shows an individuality of its own, and they all share many elements derived from the Aegeo-Anatolian mother culture. It is obvious that these connexions were stronger or weaker depending on the distance from the mother culture.

A number of imported objects from one cultural region to another show the contemporaneity and the parallel development of the cultures at Troy, Thermi and Poliochni with the Cycladic culture of the Aegean Islands and with the Early

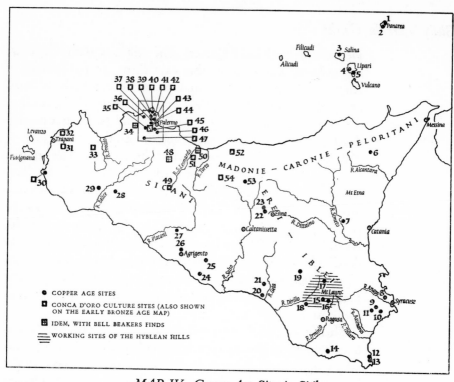

MAP IV   Copper Age Sites in Sicily

1 Piano Quartara	16 Calaforno	29 Partanna	44 Boccadifalco
2 Drauto	17 San Cono	30 Marsala	(Monte Caputo-
3 Malfa	18 Piano Arcieri	31 Paceco	Grotta Mastro
4 Piano Conte	19 San Ippolito	32 Erice	Santo-Baida)
5 Lipari acropolis	20 Piano Notaro	33 Segesta	45 Porrazzi
6 San Basilio	21 Settefarine	34 Carini	46 Villagrazia
7 Trefontane	22 Realmese	35 Monte Cuccio	47 Moarda
8 Grotta Palombara	23 Malpasso	36 Capaci	48 Villafrati
9 Grotta Chiusazza	24 Grotta Zubbia	37 Colli	49 Prizzi
10 Grotta Conzo	25 Naro	38 Valdesi	50 Termini Imerese
11 Grotta Genovese	26 Serraferlicchio	39 Monte Gallo	51 Caccamo
12 Grotta Calafarina	27 Sant' Angelo	40 Mondello	52 Isnello
13 Grotta Corruggi	Muxaro Capreria	41 Addaura	53 Grotta del
14 Grotta Maggiore	28 Santa Margherita	42 Leoni	Vecchiuzzo
15 Scalona	Belice	43 Uditore	54 Caltavuturo

63

Helladic of mainland Greece. The relations with Crete are less evident, but even in this case there are possibilities of connexions between the initial phases of the Early Minoan (Pyrgos, Aghios Onouphrios) and Poliochni III, as well as the middle phases of Troy I, which would establish a parallel development in the successive evolution in the two regions.

But this wave of civilization which brought metal techniques from the Aegean pushed westwards over the whole Mediterranean basin. Not only did it sweep over the regions which had formerly been characterized by painted pottery, such as the Italian peninsula (where the Cellino San Marco, Gaudo, Rinaldone and Remedello cultures from this time begin to develop), the Aeolian Islands and Sicily, but it also reached regions such as Sardinia, the Iberian peninsula and southern France which for so long had remained outside the progress of civilization.

There is no doubt that this expansion to lands which had once seemed so distant coincided with the new development taking place in navigation: for this, too, must now have felt the benefit of the current technical and industrial progress. During the Neolithic period navigation must have been almost exclusively coastal, and even if the Adriatic could have been traversed, by using either of the routes we have suggested in the previous chapter, the distance between Sardinia and the southern coast of Italy, Sicily, Africa and Spain must have been almost insuperable, at least to normal traffic. Accessible only by the Elba–Corsica route, the large island of Sardinia had been cut off from civilized progress, and its immense riches had never yet been exploited.

The new vessels, whose appearance has been preserved for us on Cycladic paterae, could now face the open sea with greater security, and could undertake long voyages without intermediate points of call. Sardinia, southern France and Mediterranean Spain could now easily be reached, and they suddenly move into the orbit of the civilized world and develop flourishing civilizations that continue to evolve throughout the Bronze Age.

The new sea routes linking east and west seem to have passed through the Sicilian channel rather than the Straits of Messina, reaching Sardinia by crossing between Trapani and Cagliari, and from there radiating towards the Iberian and French coasts.

Very flourishing cultures developed along this new commer⁄cial route in the Mediterranean. Malta especially, with its splendid Tarxien civilization and its extraordinary megalithic architecture, reached one of the peaks of cultural and artistic progress in prehistoric Europe. The Anghelu Ruju culture quickly developed in Sardinia, and Spain was soon to begin the Almerian culture, and France that of Fontbouïsse.

The new current of civilization which was now sweeping over the whole Mediterranean basin brought about the diffusion of new religious ideas, new funeral rites, new industrial tech⁄niques, new types of weapons and implements, new forms of pottery and new styles in its decoration.

The statue⁄stelae whose prototype comes from Troy I are now found in Malta, Corsica and southern France, and the little Cycladic marble idols are faithfully copied in Sardinia. From Anatolia to Crete, Sicily, Sardinia and Iberia the horn symbol is widely diffused: a symbol which even at this time was evidently valued as an amulet, just as it is in popular superstition today. And the apotrophaic eye symbol, which has already been noted in the neolithic Stentinello culture, also had a wide diffusion at this time from Troy to Malta, Spain and France.

The old rite of individual inhumation with the body crouched in an oval grave or in a stone cist was everywhere abandoned. This had been the exclusive rite during the Neolithic in the whole Mediterranean area, but it was now replaced by the new eastern rite of collective burial, sometimes in chamber-tombs shaped like ovens artificially cut in the ground, and sometimes in tombs built above ground and almost always in a megalithic (dolmen) tradition.

The rock-cut chamber type of tomb is undoubtedly of eastern origin: it is found in Cyprus, in the Cyclades, the Peloponnesus, Crete and Malta, and it has a very wide diffusion both in the Italian peninsula as far as the Arno (Cellino San Marco, Gaudo, Rinaldone) and in Sicily. It reached Sardinia (Anghelu Ruju), Spain and southern France.

In the west, however, the dolmen was generally preferred. This spread during the Bronze Age from Sardinia, the Iberian peninsula and southern France along the Atlantic coasts as far as the British Isles and Scandinavia.

The rite of inhumation in a large jar also originated in the east (Troy, Yortan), though it appeared sporadically in the west at a somewhat later date, in the Bronze Age in Sicily (Milazzo), Lipari and Spain (El Argar).

Among the stone weapons and implements introduced by the new civilization, the most characteristic are the battle axes and the perforated mace-heads, ovoid, spherical or pear-shaped. Both these types were widely diffused in the Troy and Poliochni civilizations, and are found again, though more sporadically, in the western Mediterranean. The battle axe, though present in the Italian peninsula (Rinaldone), is not known from Sicily, but the mace-head is represented by a large number of examples.

In the bone industry, too, there are some characteristic types which spread westwards from the east during the Copper Age and the beginning of the Bronze Age. These include not only the plaques decorated with little incised circles (Troy, Poliochni, Melilli, Anghelu Ruju) but, above all, the extraordinary bossed bone objects, probably schematized idols. These are found not only in Troy but in the Peloponnesus (Lerna), Malta and Sicily, where they were very popular in the Castelluccio culture.

As far as the pottery is concerned, it would take us too far off our course to follow the diffusion of forms, techniques and decorative motifs from their East Mediterranean prototypes in the cultures of Troy, Poliochni, the Cyclades and Cyprus, into the far west. There are forms which clearly have an eastern origin, and these include jugs with cut-away necks, necked or hour-glass mugs, mugs with handle linking the base with a very high raised triangular lug on the rim, spouted vessels, duck-shaped askoi, beak-handled bases, polypod vases, etc.

In not one of the central and western Mediterranean cultures that we think were influenced from the east do we find all these Aegeo-Anatolian features combined, but a few were adopted by each culture. As a matter of fact, it often happens that some of these elements seem to be absent in the early phases of these regional cultures, and that they then make a sudden appearance much later, and have a wider diffusion than they would have done at first. It is obvious that in such cases they were not self-engendered; on the contrary, even if our knowledge is still too fragmentary for us to have very precise evidence about them, we should regard these elements as being part of the cultural heritage of the Copper Age peoples from the beginning of the period.

Everything leads us to believe, however, that the historical phenomena which we have just described were the outcome not of a sudden but of a gradual process, perhaps lasting over several centuries.

There must have been a considerable lapse of time between the point when the Aegeo-Anatolian cultures began to play a predominant part in the cultural and economic development of the eastern and central Mediterranean, and the point when we can consider the Copper Age cultures of Sardinia, the Iberian peninsula and southern France as being complete in their essential characteristics and able in their turn to radiate and transmit cultural impulses farther afield.

It is obvious that the main stream of cultural influence from Anatolia was not the only one to contribute to the formation of Mediterranean civilization: there were others whose interven⁄tion added many complications to the scene. Sometimes there are developments, survivals or revivals of earlier local cultures; sometimes there are new cultural contributions coming by various routes such as those from eastern Europe, and above all from the Danube valley; there are ethnical factors, environ⁄mental factors, and, last but not least, there is the individuality and the creative spirit of Man himself.

Each of the derivative cultures has therefore its own indivi⁄duality: particular characteristics differentiating it from the near⁄by cultures, and allowing us sometimes to distinguish the separate phases in its evolution. Each has, in fact, its own internal evolution in which it is already possible in some cases to outline fairly clearly the successive advances.

This evolution is particularly important in the Iberian penin⁄sula, where the new Copper Age civilization, initially perhaps rooted in Almeria, spread quickly over the whole peninsula. As a result of fruitful hybridization with the local substratum, it gave rise to the splendid bell⁄beaker culture which radiated over the whole of western Europe and became one of the most active progressive factors.

The cultural elements characterizing this Iberian bell⁄beaker culture (the bell⁄beaker itself, V⁄bored buttons, big flint daggers and flint arrow⁄heads with careful retouches over the whole surface, etc.) spread widely not only over the western Mediter⁄ranean as far as Sardinia, the Italian mainland, Sicily and Malta, but also over a large part of continental Europe. It reached the Rhine and Danube valleys as well as the British Isles, and so witnessed to the cultural and economic pre⁄eminence which the Iberian peninsula had rapidly achieved in the west.

I. THE COPPER AGE IN THE AEOLIAN ISLANDS

In the Aeolian Islands the Copper Age seems to have been a period of poverty and decadence.

The trade in obsidian which had been the source of prosperity during the Neolithic was gradually failing owing to the rapid progress in metallurgy in the central and western Mediterranean. The principal trade routes by sea now seem to

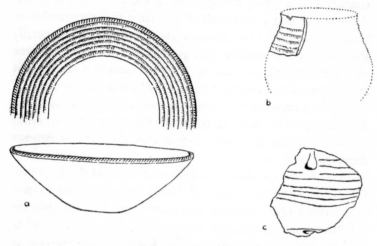

Fig. 7   Channelled ware of the Piano Conte style:
(a) from Piano Conte (Diam. 13");
(b, c) from the Lipari acropolis.
Lipari Museum.

have passed not through the Straits of Messina but rather through the Sicilian channel, with Malta in particular as the focal-point.

We can recognize two distinct stages in the Copper Age evolution in the Aeolian Islands, and we can perhaps glimpse signs of a third stage, little known so far.

We have called the first stage after Piano Conte, the village in the locality of that name in the uplands of Lipari, though other levels of this cultural *facies* are also found at other points in the island.

On the acropolis and in the Diana plain the levels belonging to this time immediately overlie those of the neolithic Diana style, from which they are, however, completely different.

One has the impression that there was a total change in the civilization of the islands. The pottery is now of a brown, coarsely baked paste, though with a glossy surface; it is un-decorated or may have bands of very large shallow grooves, or sometimes burnished striations made with a spatula. Generally there are no real handles, but perforated bosses and in some cases tubular lugs not built up from the surface of the pot but subcutaneously; these are generally called 'tunnel handles'.

Fig. 7, a, b   The forms are few: the most common are the shallow bowls decorated inside, and globular or pear-shaped jars, while carinated bowls are rare. Big coarse pots are sometimes decorated with cordons.

These forms are closely analogous to those of the Lagozza-Chassey-Cortaillod cultures of North Italy, southern France, Switzerland and Catalonia. But some of the elements, like the

Fig. 7, c   subcutaneous handles and the grooved decoration, seem to be later and related rather to the Copper Age cultures of Rinaldone, Anghelu Ruju and Fontbouïsse.

In our present state of knowledge the Piano Conte culture might be regarded as one of the last offsprings of the Lagozza-Chassey-Cortaillod cultures, and already under the influences of the Copper Age cultures which were by this time becoming established in the surrounding regions.

As far as relations with Sicily are concerned, it is a very interesting fact that in the levels of the Piano Conte culture there are found fragments of imported painted pottery in the Serraferlicchio style. Moreover, the burnished decoration made with a spatula has parallels in a well-known class of Sicilian pottery belonging to the Early Copper Age, and certainly descended from prototypes in the Rachmani-Larissa-Eutresis cultures of continental Greece.

The second Aeolian cultural *facies* is the Piano Quartara one. First identified in 1946 at the site of that name in the island of

Fig. 8   Characteristic pottery forms of the Piano Quartara style from the neighbourhood of Diana in Lipari. Height of large pot 6¾", others to scale. Lipari Museum.

Panarea, this culture was not represented in the stratigraphical series on the Lipari acropolis, and accordingly its cultural position was very uncertain. Recently, however, levels very characteristic of this *facies* have been found in the stratigraphy of the Diana plain: these overlie the Piano Conte strata and are below those of the Early Bronze Age (Capo Graziano culture).

We still know very little about the Piano Quartara culture. The curious 'sauce-boats' which characterize it have very vague analogies with those of the Early Helladic on the Greek main-land; but the elbow-shaped handles with pointed tips on these 'sauce-boats' have parallels in the Copper Age cultures of the

Fig. 8

Italian mainland (Cellino San Marco near Brindisi, the Polada lake-dwellings in Lombardy).

We shall see how identical types are found again in Sicily, especially in the area of expansion of the Conca d'Oro culture.

The absence of the Piano Quartara cultural *facies* in the stratigraphy of the Lipari acropolis shows that, at least for some while, this rock was uninhabited. Theoretically, therefore, there may also be other prehistoric Aeolian cultures unrepresented there. Actually some pots which constituted the grave-goods of two tombs, and which came respectively from Malfa in the island of Salina and from Drauto in Panarea, belong to a type not yet known from Lipari. They have, however, close analogies with objects from a collective tomb at Andria in Apulia, some vases of which seem to be precursors of the types characteristic of the Bronze Age in that district.

2. THE COPPER AGE IN SICILY

The cultural panorama in Sicily at this period appears to have been unusually complex. Earlier excavations had made it possible to identify many pottery types, each one of which has well-marked characteristics of style and technique. But until now it had been very difficult to understand properly the cultural significance of each of these, and it was impossible to be sure whether they represented co-existing or succeeding cultural *facies*.

The materials of this period kept in the museums of Syracuse and Palermo are by now very considerable: there are deposits like those of Zubbia at Palma di Montechiaro, of Serrafer-licchio, of Sant' Ippolito at Caltagirone, of Trefontane at Paternò, of the Grotta del Vecchiuzzo at Petralia Sottana, which have produced really outstanding quantities of pottery. In each of them, however, the different types were associated in different ways: one had the impression that each of these sites must have passed through several cultural phases. But, as we have said, it was, above all, not possible to establish a chronological succession of types, owing either to the lack of a clear strati/ graphy or to the lack of systematic method in the excavations.

In the last few months, however, the scientific excavation of the Grotta della Chiusazza, seven miles from Syracuse on the road to Canicattini, has produced a stratigraphic basis for establishing the relative chronology at least of the pottery types represented there. We will therefore describe this cave in more detail.

3. THE GROTTA DELLA CHIUSAZZA AND THE OTHER CAVES IN THE CANICATTINI DISTRICT

Between Syracuse and Canicattini there is a region in which there are numerous large caves, sometimes of extraordinary beauty from a spelaeological point of view.

The Grotta della Chiusazza, one of the biggest of these, is certainly the richest archaeologically. In spite of the extremely stony nature of the soil in some places in this cave, it has produced a very clear stratigraphy which we can summarize here, beginning with the upper levels.

1. Greek period, with signs that there was a cult in the cave, which was regarded as sacred.
2. Middle Bronze Age level, with pottery of Thapsos style.
3. Early Bronze Age level, with painted pottery of Castel/ luccio style.
4. Late Copper Age level, with red pottery of Malpasso style and with coarse pottery of red, yellowish or light/ coloured paste, undecorated.
5. Middle Copper Age, with coarse pottery like the level above and with pottery painted in opaque black on a light reddish or purplish ground, in the Serraferlicchio style.

6. Early Copper Age, with the following classes of pottery:

(a) Painted pottery of Conzo style with red bands bordered in black, forming panels filled with hatched black triangles on a yellowish ground.

(b) Buccheroid grey ware decorated with burnished lines.

(c) Pottery of brown paste with decoration incised before firing in the San Cono-Piano Notaro style and represented here by only a few fragments.

7. Lowest levels with red Diana style pottery.

The distinction between the Early Copper Age level 6 and the Middle Copper Age level 5 is not in reality a very clear one. The types from the earlier level seem sometimes to last on into the later one. There is a more marked distinction between the levels of the Middle and Late Copper Age in spite of the continuation of coarse ware. Also common to these two last levels is a remarkable number of clay or pottery objects: votive horns, flat or biconical spindle-whorls, simple disc lids without knobs but with side-perforations.

The near-by Grotta del Conzo, where all the pottery types of the Early, Middle and Late Copper Age were mixed without any stratigraphical distinction, also produced a beautiful globular mace-head with cylindrical perforation. It was made of marble of a type well known at Troy, though so far only very few examples have been found in Sicily (Grotta del Fico at Isnello, Valdesi, Cefalù).

Deposits of the same age come from another near-by cave, the Grotta Genovese, and from a fourth cave, La Palombara, at Targia, a few miles to the north of Syracuse.

The excavations of the Chiusazza cave, though still in the early stages and confined to a limited area, have already yielded some interesting results. In fact, they enable us to establish the relative chronology of some of the main pottery types of this period and to recognize at least three very distinct and charac-teristic phases in the evolution of the Sicilian Copper Age. The Copper Age, however, still remains the least well-known period of Sicilian prehistory, and we cannot find a satisfactory answer to many of the problems concerning the deposits of this time.

We shall see in the course of an examination of the individual deposits that they may have other types of pottery than those represented at Chiusazza. We shall see in particular that Sicily did not at this time have one single culture, but that we can distinguish at least two large cultural provinces, one taking in the eastern, central and southern parts and the other the north of the island.

Let us examine the different pottery types of this period, in the chronological order in which they appear in the Chiusazza stratigraphy, and at the same time take a quick glance at the principal deposits in which each of them has been found.

4. THE POTTERY OF SAN CONO-PIANO NOTARO STYLE

The village of San Cono, made known by the brothers Corrado and Ippolito Cafici, was situated on the top of a hill, which, though not very steep or high, lay in an isolated position, half-way between Vizzini and Licodia in the Hyblaean Hills.

In this village, which has not so far been chosen for specific excavation, only slight indications of huts could be recognized, but potsherds, querns and rubbers—above all, an extraordin-arily abundant stone industry—were collected from this site.

Close by the village two tombs of very different types were discovered. The first was a round grave covered with irregular stone slabs; it was therefore a tomb still of the neolithic type comparable with one of the Stentinello period at Calaforno, and others at Molfetta in Apulia. The second tomb, on the contrary, was of the oven type, opening out from the bottom of a small cylindrical shaft: this is a Copper Age type which we shall find widely diffused in the Conca d'Oro culture.

In 1908 Paolo Orsi published a group of tombs discovered at Gela on the Iozza estate in the Piano Notaro locality. These were round graves surrounded with vertical stone slabs, and contained crouched skeletons: they produced the most outstanding group of pottery in this style so far brought to light.

Plates 18, 19

Fig. 9, d, g

Fig. 9, a–c

Pottery of a style completely analogous to the Piano Notaro ware made up by far the greatest part of the finds from the Grotta Zubbia at Palma di Montechiaro. A few painted sherds were mixed with them.

The same might be said of the material from the Grotta Calafarina near Pachino, the levels of which had unfortunately been badly disturbed by treasure-hunters. Orsi, however, was still able to find some undisturbed burials in a recess.

At Sant' Ippolito near Caltagirone and at Trefontane near Paternò, pottery of San Cono style was mixed with some of both earlier and later date.

A small vase from Ossini near Militello, in the plain of Catania, has a decoration scratched after firing and is strictly analogous to some vases from Piano Notaro. Only one pot in the San Cono style was found among the material at Serraferlicchio (Agrigento).

The pottery of San Cono-Piano Notaro style is not very different in quality from the undecorated ware of Stentinello. It is, in fact, of a fine paste, well fired, well smoothed and polished, with a monochrome grey or blackish surface.

As a rule it is not decorated but sometimes has fine lines incised before firing, often with pairs of curved lines or with lines bordered with little impressed dots, outlining large panels.

Plate 19

Bowl-like impressions are not rare. The incisions are often emphasized by incrustation with a white substance or with red ochre. Decoration scratched after firing is rather rare, though not altogether absent. Sometimes there is a decoration painted in red ochre on the dark background of the pot; it is generally confined to a few bands outlined by incised lines, but in some cases it covers the whole surface of the pot.

There are not many very common types: carinated or trun-cated conical bowls, carinated cups, jars more or less ovoid,

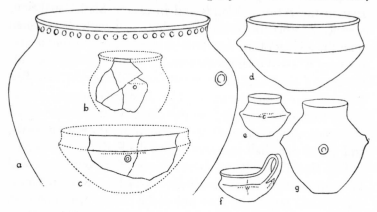

Fig. 9   Characteristic pottery forms of the San Cono-Piano Notaro style:
(a–c) from Grotta Zubbia at Palma di Montechiaro;
(d–g) tombs at Gela, Piano Notaro. Height of (e) 6⅜", others to scale.
Syracuse Museum.

though sometimes these too are carinated, and some small pithoi. Other forms such as the one-handled dippers are rarer.

Real handles are usually not found; in their place there are simple pierced bosses or slight lugs. A number of earthenware objects such as spindle-whorls, weights and spoons are by now found with this pottery. Actually, the pottery, both in its types and in some of its forms, seems to be strictly related to that of the Stentinello culture. The same may be said of the incised decoration which could have been a very simplified derivation from the rich Stentinello decoration. There are motifs at Sten-tinello itself, in fact, which might be the origin of the ones more frequently used in the San Cono pottery.

Fig. 10 Big painted jar from the Grotta della Chiusazza (Syracuse). Height 23½". Syracuse Museum

The scratched decoration which did not appear at Stentinello is certainly, however, a contribution from the Apulo-Materan cultures, where it is often found associated with painted ware. But this relationship between the San Cono-Piano Notaro pottery and that of Stentinello (much more than with that of the painted pottery which, as we have seen, succeeded it, at least in the Aeolian Islands and in eastern Sicily) makes us wonder whether the Stentinello culture had really disappeared with the advent of the new foreign cultures, or whether it may not have lingered on for some time in the parts of Sicily outside the area of their expansion, finally engendering the new San Cono-Piano Notaro culture. The decorative motifs of San Cono-Piano Notaro are, on the contrary, still those which characterize the Conca d'Oro culture of north-western Sicily, and which we shall see survive until the Early Bronze Age.

The San Cono-Piano Notaro style of decoration would seem, therefore, to have lasted for a very long time in Sicily, and in some respects to have linked the earliest Neolithic with the Early Bronze Age. Thus, it seems to have been the expression of an indigenous element which succeeded in retaining its individuality and its characteristics over many centuries and through a long series of ethnical and cultural vicissitudes.

5. THE PAINTED POTTERY OF CONZO AND THE BURNISH DECORATED WARE

Fig. 10

The other classes of pottery found in the lower levels of Chiusazza are so far much less well known in Sicily. The painted pottery with big panels of red bands outlined in black and with a series of hatched triangles on the yellowish inner ground is so far known only from Chiusazza and the near-by Grotta del Conzo. No other examples are known.

The shape of the panels formed by the painted lines is

peculiarly reminiscent of the commonest decorative motifs of
the incised pottery of San Cono-Piano Notaro style. Plate 18

Actually this painted Conzo pottery shows an undeniable
resemblance to the pottery with red bands bordered with black
which characterized the early levels of the Middle Neolithic on
the Lipari acropolis. But this is a superficial analogy, since the Plates 16, 17
neolithic pottery was much finer and glossy, and it also had a
variety of types and forms. The Conzo ware, on the contrary,
is opaque and coarse both in make and design; furthermore,
the vessels are reduced almost to a single form, a big pear-
shaped jar without handles or only with mean little handles,
which becomes monotonous.

The possibility of the derivation of one class from the other
cannot be excluded, however. One should, moreover, consider
the possibility of a long survival of this element in a culturally
stagnant and isolated area (a phenomenon similar to the persistence we have suggested in connexion with the incised pottery
of San Cono style).

As for the buccheroid ware from these caves in the Syracuse
neighbourhood, it is found again, in forms which, even if
not identical, are at least closely akin to it, at Serraferlicchio Plate 22
just outside Agrigento, i.e. at the extreme opposite side of
Sicily.

One simple but very typical example was also found at
Trefontane (Paternò) on the slopes of Etna. Plate 21

If the forms differ in some respects at Chiusazza and Serraferlicchio (at this latter site big truncated conical bowls with three
or four large handles are commonest, whereas at Chiusazza
there are bowls, more rounded in shape and handleless), the
burnished decoration of vertical, often interrupted, striations
made with a spatula, is everywhere identical. It is, in fact, the
same decoration as we have already noticed at Lipari in the
Piano Conte culture.

One is really dealing with a technique of decoration which

had its origins in the Aegean and makes its appearance in the Rachmani period, i.e. at the end of the Greek Neolithic.

6. THE PAINTED POTTERY OF SERRAFERLICCHIO STYLE

The site of Serragerlicchio is just outside Agrigento, in a big mountain cleft, in which an enormous quantity of pottery has been found. All around are small cavities and near by one can recognize a few traces of huts.

Amongst this mass of pottery sundry classes, probably not all contemporaneous, can be distinguished. The excavator of Serraferlicchio (Arias) noted that the painted ware which is most typical of this site was absent in the lower levels, and this fact coincides well with what we have observed at Chiusazza. We have already noted the single cup, with scratched decora∕ tion in the San Cono style, which came from Serraferlicchio, and the abundant buccheroid ware, including large bowls and jars.

But, above all, Serraferlicchio had produced (apart from rather rare varieties) a characteristic pottery painted in opaque black on a shiny bright red or purplish∕red ground, which is the one we shall call after this site.

Plate 24

Fig. 11

This ware is very varied in shape and includes pots of all sizes, from the largest to the smallest. The motifs, too, are as varied: chevron bands, groups of lines, big dots, wavy lines, hatched panels, hour∕glass motifs, etc.; and they are intermixed in a very lively and unexpected way.

Among the commonest and most characteristic motifs are those consisting of groups of parallel lines alternating in various

Fig. 11, b

directions and one with thin vertical bands from which narrow elongated wedges slant out obliquely; in between there are wavy lines.

At Serraferlicchio there are also a few examples of a poli-chrome ware, in which the black bands on a bright red ground are bordered with white bands or alternate with them. It is this type that we shall find again at Trefontane near Paternò and at Sant' Ippolito near Caltagirone. It must therefore belong to

*Fig. 11   Painted pottery from the site of Serraferlicchio (Agrigento). Height of (d) 5½",
others to scale.
Syracuse Museum.*

a slightly later period than the one characterized by the black or red ware.

Also represented at Serraferlicchio, though not abundantly, is the monochrome ware of Malpasso style, similar in all respects to forms from the Late Copper Age levels at Chiusazza. At Serraferlicchio, too, this seems to be later than the other classes of pottery. Lastly, there is a great mass of coarse pottery exactly like that from the Middle and Later Copper Ages at Chiusazza, both in the light colour of its paste and in its simple decoration limited to a few cordons or bosses.

The black or red pottery characteristic of Serraferlicchio has not been found on a number of other sites scattered almost all over Sicily. We find it right in the heart of the island on an open site in the Realmese fee near Calascibetta, a site which

Fig. 12   Vase painted in black and red from Capaci. Palermo Museum.

must originally have been on the top of a hill, but whose material was washed down by rainwater into the little valley below.

In the Syracuse district it is found not only in the Chiusazza cave but also in the Grotta Genovese close by, and in the Grotta Palombara at Targia.

A typical but isolated pot in this style was found at Paternò. A few fragments of it came from Lipari in the levels belonging to the Piano-Conte culture, and provide us with very important data for the synchronization of the Aeolian cultures with those of Sicily.

A sensibly different variant—not in its technique, which is always much the same, but in its decorative motifs—comes from the Grotta del Vecchiuzzo at Petralia Sottana. One pot from this cave, published by Signora Marconi Bovio, bears the unusual motif of a big angular pattern made with a group of thin lines, and by bordering lines of little triangular 'pennants': this is a motif which is not known from Serraferlicchio, though it is found on a little pot from a tomb at Capaci near Palermo, and is so far the only example of this style brought to light in the diffusion area of the Conca d'Oro culture.

Fig. 12

The pottery of Serraferlicchio style, both in its technique of decoration and in its form, still seems to fit into the last phases of the Greek Neolithic, i.e. both genetically and typologically it precedes the Early Helladic.

7. THE MONOCHROME RED WARE OF THE MALPASSO STYLE

Near Calascibetta, in the middle of Sicily, in a locality known as Malpasso, a few miles from Realmese, five tombs were dis﹣ covered a few years ago: they are of the chamber type, cut into the soft limestone, but somewhat different from the oven type, which we shall see was more widely diffused in Sicily in the Bronze Age. They are, in fact, tombs with several little intercommunicating rooms.

Fig. 13 Plan of the rock﹣cut tomb in the Malpasso necropolis near Calascibetta (Enna). Width of chamber, 15 ft.

The pottery found in them all has a monochrome red surface, and comprises only a few types. Most characteristic is the semi﹣ oval mug with a big strip handle linking a slightly protruding base to a large vertical triangular projection built up on the rim and sometimes surmounted by an axe﹣like terminal.

Fig. 14

This type of pottery is also present with more varieties of form at Serraferlicchio, and in the Grotta del Vecchiuzzo at Petralia Sottana, but above all in the Sant' Ippolito site near Caltagirone.

There is no doubt that here it corresponds strictly to that which characterizes the upper levels of the Grotta della

Fig. 14 Characteristic forms of monochrome red ware of Malpasso style:
(a–c) from the Malpasso tombs;
(d) from the Grotta del Vecchiuzzo;
(e) provenance unknown. Height of (b) 8″, others to scale.
Syracuse Museum (a, c, e); Palermo Museum (d).

Chiusazza. In this case, too, the wide distribution of this type of pottery excludes the possibility of considering it only as a local aspect.

We no longer find analogies for these forms in the Late Aegean Neolithic, as in the case of both the burnish decorated buccheroid ware and the painted Serraferlicchio pottery: this time the parallels come quite definitely from the Early Bronze Age of Anatolia. The typical mugs with upraised triangular projections are clearly reminiscent of examples from Alishar and Kültepe.

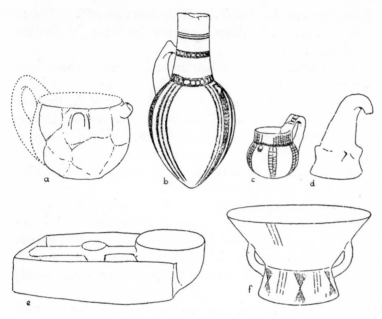

*Fig. 15   Characteristic forms of pottery from the site of Sant' Ippolito (Caltagirone).
Height of (b) 10", others to scale. Syracuse Museum.*

8. THE SITE OF SANT' IPPOLITO AND ITS PAINTED POTTERY

The site on the Sant' Ippolito (or Guardia, or Bersaglio) hill at Caltagirone is another of the most important deposits in Copper Age Sicily.

Here was found a large quantity of pottery ranging in date from the Neolithic to the Early Iron Age; actually the site represents a number of villages either juxtaposed or super-imposed one upon the other. Pottery of the Stentinello type, perhaps only of its final phases, was found here, and two or three scroll handles of pinkish-buff clay seem to belong to the spiral-meander style of Serra d'Alto. There is also pottery with

85

incised lines bordered with dots in the San Cono-Piano Notaro style. But the predominant types seem to belong to the later stages of the Copper Age.

The relationships with Serraferlicchio seem to have been closest at a period which we are led to believe was the latest, the final one of this site. In fact, while many of the forms of coarse ware are common to both sites, the classes characterizing the earliest and middle phases at Serraferlicchio (as, for instance, the buccheroid ware and the one painted in black and red) are absent at Sant' Ippolito or appear in very different (or more evolved) forms than at Serraferlicchio.

Some types are frequently found here which were rare at Serraferlicchio, like the polychrome pottery with black bands bordered in white on a red ground, and the little pithoi or cups decorated with irregular black lines on a yellowish ground. The monochrome red ware of Malpasso type is also widely represented.

Fig. 15

But the most characteristic ware at Sant' Ippolito is a kind of pottery, almost always painted, that more than any other class of Sicilian pottery reveals the direct derivation of its forms from Aegeo-Anatolian prototypes. This is shown mainly by the one-handled mugs and the small two-handled pots, more

Fig. 15, c

or less spherical in shape and with a low cylindrical neck, which are by far the commonest forms, but particularly by

Fig. 15, b

the little high-necked ovoid flasks of specifically Cypriot type.

As in the case of its oriental prototypes, the mouth of the Sant' Ippolito specimen is cut obliquely.

Fig. 15, a

There was also an unpainted hemispherical tubular spouted jug which has parallels all over the Aegean and especially in Crete. There are fruit dishes as well, on high conical stands, sometimes with one or two handles between the stand and the

Fig. 15, f

dish, and lastly some very curious oval, or rectangular, basin-like containers with a hemispherical cup inserted into one side,

which is joined to the opposite side of the basin by a little
central bridge of unknown significance.   *Fig. 15,* e

The decoration of this pottery painted in a dark colour on a
yellowish or reddish background is very simple and belongs to
a rigid decorative conception.

On the necks of the little pots are groups of horizontal or
vertical lines, triangles, or sometimes big dots. Below the
shoulder there are spaced groups of three vertical lines or angles
made with crossed lines.

An absolutely identical complex to that of Sant' Ippolito
comes from the hut-village of Settefarine near Gela, but little
flasks of Cypriot type exactly like the one from Sant' Ippolito
have been found in the Gela district (Caltagirone Museum)
and at Villafrati near Palermo.

The fact that this type of pottery is unrepresented in the
Chiusazza cave, and only indicated or, perhaps, we should
say, heralded by a few elements at Serraferlicchio, seems to
show that it may have developed fully only after this site had
ceased to be used.

The Sant' Ippolito pottery may be characteristic of an even
later period than that of the red Malpasso ware.

9. THE CONCA D'ORO CULTURE OF NORTH-WESTERN SICILY

North-western Sicily, that is to say the region consisting of the
modern provinces of Palermo and Trapani, seems to have been
very different from the rest of Sicily at this period.

The culture which flourished here has been called the 'Conca
d'Oro culture' by Signora Marconi Bovio, who has described
its characteristics, because most of the sites in which it is represented are in Palermo itself or in its immediate surroundings
(via Roma, Porrazzi, Boccadifalco, Valdesi, Mondello, Baida,

Sant' Isidoro, Uditore, Piazza Leoni, Parco della Favorita), and in a rather wider strip around the Conca d'Oro (Villafrati, Moarda, Capaci, Carini). Farther away in western Sicily (Segesta, Erice, Paceco, Motya, Marsala, Partanna, Santa Margherita Belice, Prizzi) and on the Tyrrhenian coast to the east of Palermo (caves at Termini Imerese, Caccamo, Calta- vuturo, Isnello), the finds have hitherto been fewer; but this may be the result of less intensive research. This culture is chiefly, though not exclusively, known from grave-goods.

Fig. 16   The tombs are consistently of the oven type, opening out from a little vertical shaft: a type, namely, of Aegeo-Anatolian origin. Sometimes one shaft may lead to two or even three sepulchral cells. The diameter of these is seldom more than six feet, and sometimes less than three feet. In every cell there are several crouched burials with vases, weapons, objects of stone, earthenware and bone, occasionally of metal, which were placed around them as grave-goods. Frequently, powdered ochre is found in these tombs. Natural as well as rock-cut caves were used for burial places.

The decorated pottery can be divided into two distinct groups, one constituted by the real and proper Conca d'Oro style, and the other by the Moarda style ware. Many elements lead us to think that this may, at least genetically, be more evolved than the Conca d'Oro style. But the two types are sometimes associated in one tomb and the undecorated ware usually seems to be common to the two groups.

In the stylistic group of the Conca d'Oro proper, almost the only decoration consists of incised lines, sometimes in pairs, and often bordered with a row of impressed dots forming panels. It is a decoration that we have, in fact, already met in eastern Sicily, in the San Cono-Piano Notaro culture.

The vase shapes, however, are largely different: with rare exceptions they are globular jars without real handles but with simple perforated bosses, small one-handled mugs and thin vases. A very significant type is the 'Carini beaker', a local imitation of the bell-beaker, but decorated in the typical Conca d'Oro style. The shapes of the plain ware are much more varied and show a number of influences. Some seem to continue the San ConoPiano Notaro tradition and even that of Stentinello, but the most typical forms of the San Cono culture,

Plate 25

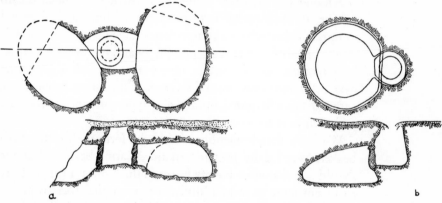

Fig. 16   Two ovenshaped and shaft tombs of the Conca d'Oro culture type: (a) Palermo (Uditore); (b) Capaci. Diameter of tomb (b), 12 ft.

for example the big carinated bowls characteristic of the Piano Notaro tombs and Grotta Zubbia no longer appear.

Fig. 9, c, d

Other forms repeat those that are known from the painted pottery at Serraferlicchio, but a good many by now clearly show the influence of derived AegeoAnatolian forms, of the red Malpasso style ware and of painted Sant' Ippolito pottery. Of these we find in particular the collared mug, the flask with very high cylindrical neck, some small amphorae, some dippercups with very long, curved handles, etc. A painted flask from Villafrati seems to be a real import from the Sant' Ippolito cultural horizon in eastcentral Sicily. Some pots with oval mouths or with big elbowhandles terminating in pointed projections closely resemble those from the Aeolian culture of

Fig. 17

Piano Quartara. But some little vases found at Villafrati and at Moarda exactly reproduce types characteristic of another Aeolian culture, that of Capo Graziano, now representing the Early Bronze Age in Lipari. Considering their relative isolation in the complex of the Palermo area, there is every likelihood that they were actually imported from the Aeolian Islands.

Among the imported elements to reach the Conca d'Oro culture, the bellbeaker is of fundamental interest, and several examples either whole or fragmentary have now been found in Sicily. Actually, the wellknown examples from Villafrati have recently been joined by others from a tomb at Partanna near Selinunte, while from the Grotta Chiusilla at Isnello there comes a bone Vbored button of a type constantly associated with bellbeakers in the Iberian peninsula.

We have already mentioned that the form itself of the bellbeakers was locally imitated in the 'Carini beaker'. But we should add that other pottery forms in the Conca d'Oro culture also seem more or less faithfully to have copied Iberian prototypes belonging to the same cultural horizon as the bellbeakers.

All this goes to show the profoundly eclectic character of the Conca d'Oro culture, towards which very diverse influences seem to have converged. They came not only from southeastern Sicily and the Aeolian Islands but also from faroff Iberia. Moreover, these influences seem to have been imposed on an indigenous, strongly conservative cultural background where techniques and decorative pottery styles already traditional in Sicily were perpetuated; styles like those which, perhaps evolving from late Stentinello motifs, characterized the San ConoPiano Notaro culture.

One has the impression, therefore, that in Sicily an indigenous cultural nucleus continued to exist, untouched by the advent of new, foreign cultures, which perhaps affected only limited parts of the island. Side by side with the paintedpottery culture of the Middle and Late Neolithic (which eastern Sicily at least had shared with the Aeolian Islands and southern Italy) and with the Copper Age cultures of overseas origin (e.g. Serraferlicchio, Malpasso, Sant' Ippolito), there seems also to have been a local indigenous culture. It was influenced to some extent by the former, but in the main continued faithful to the Stentinello tradition which it perpetuated.

Fig. 17 Pottery of the Capo Graziano style, from tombs of the Conca d'Oro culture type: (a, b) from Villafrati; (c) from Moarda. (Height (a) and (b) about 4".) Palermo Museum.

In fact, while all the other decorative styles that alternated in Sicily seem to have had only a short duration, and have disappeared as soon as a new style established itself, the decorative style of San Cono and Conca d'Oro carried on the motifs which had already been used on Stentinello pottery and which seem to have lasted for a very long time. Whereas we find it represented in the lowest levels of the Chiusazza cave at the beginning of the Copper Age, at Villafrati it is associated with bell-beakers and with pottery in the Aeolian Capo Graziano style, in the Early Bronze Age.

The funeral rite has changed from the oval single-graves of Piano Notaro and the first San Cono tomb, to the oven tombs with shaft and chamber, which are exclusive at this time to the Conca d'Oro. Although the implements and pottery forms have undergone various influences from the fresh influxes of population, the basic decorative motifs remain unchanged.

10. THE MOARDA STYLE POTTERY OF THE CONCA D'ORO CULTURE

Among the several tombs in the Conca d'Oro culture, and above all in those of Moarda, Segesta, Torrebigini and Isnello, there are some which produce examples of a totally different kind of pottery from the usual characteristic type.

Plates 26, 27   It is a very fine ware, much more richly and attractively ornamented. The decoration consists of lines incised before firing and in the main comprises parallel bands or zones, hatched or criss-crossed, sometimes making multiple angles and Plate 23   also simple groups of incised parallel lines.

Both in its technique and its motifs this pottery seems to be a dim reflection of the bell-beaker style decoration in the Iberian peninsula, though it also has analogies, which can hardly be accidental, with the pottery of the Sardinian Copper Age from Anghelu Ruju and Marinaru. Both these sites are also related to the Iberian bell-beaker culture.

The Conca d'Oro culture must have been of very long duration: it must have been developing right through the Copper Age and have gone on during the whole Early Bronze Age when the Capo Graziano culture was already established in the Aeolian Islands, and the Castelluccio culture in south-eastern Sicily. Pots typical of these two cultures were, in fact, associated in the Villafrati and Torrebigini tombs with Conca d'Oro ware.

It must have corresponded with a period of unusual prosperity in north-western Sicily: a prosperity due, no doubt, chiefly to traffic with the distant west, with Sardinia and the Iberian peninsula, whose importance is attested by the bell-beakers and the local imitations of the beakers themselves and of their style of decoration.

There seems no doubt that these relations with the west

developed in the last phases of the Conca d'Oro culture, since the bell-beakers so far known are associated with the Capo Graziano style (Villafrati) and the West Castelluccio style (Torrebigini). The Moarda ware, derived from bell-beakers, would therefore appear to be the ultimate product of this Sicilian culture.

II. IMPLEMENTS OF THE SICILIAN COPPER AGE

While in the case of the pottery—which almost always has a very distinct decorative style—it has been possible to establish not only its typological but also its chronological position, it is much more difficult to do this with the other classes of objects from the Sicilian sites of this period; we prefer therefore to consider them as a whole.

Some of these sites, specially Sant' Ippolito near Caltagirone, have produced a great variety of objects. Characteristic of this period are the terra-cotta horns, which certainly had a prophy-lactic value and as amulets are still valued in popular supersti-tion, especially in southern Italy. But there are many classes of terra-cotta objects of practical use: spindle-whorls (generally spherical or biconical, less often cylindrical, discoidal or bun-shaped), reels, spoons, weights of various forms, lids of simple disc shape with holes near the edge, or of a conical type surmounted by a knob.

Metal, too, is certainly known by this time, but only a few objects have been found. Almost all of them come from burials of the Conca d'Oro *facies*, and therefore belong to the Early Bronze Age: a single little dagger and a bracelet from Chiusilla at Isnello, a little ring from Boccadifalco, and small fragments from Sant' Isidoro.

The stone industry is very varied: so far the axe hammer or battle axe is unknown from Sicily, though there are examples of these in the contemporaneous culture of the Italian mainland (Rinaldone). But there are some axes with cylindrical perforation. One very wellmade specimen came from Palazzolo Acreide.

Some maceheads are, however, known from Sicily, both globular and oval ones, with cylindrical perforation of a type well known at Troy and in Egypt. Specimens were recovered from the Grotta del Fico at Isnello, from Valdesi and Cefalù, and a recent discovery has added another, already mentioned, from the Grotta del Conzo (Syracuse).

Polished axes are very common; the largest ones, generally biconvex, are almost always made of basalt while the better examples, made of hard greenstone, are rather rare. The smaller, often diminutive ones are almost always made of greenstone, quite frequently planoconvex, and many of them have a perforated butt. Querns, rubbers and pestles are common everywhere.

Arrowheads retouched on both sides, which have been known since the neolithic Diana style, are now very widely diffused. But in Sicily the hollowbased type is almost exclusive: the leafshaped and barbed and tanged types are much rarer.

Blades with rounded tips and marginal retouching are common; so, too, are endscrapers.

Proper flintdaggers with retouching on two facets in the Solutrean technique like those in the Iberian peninsula, in southern France, and the Italian cultures of Remedello, Rinaldone, Gaudo, are unknown from Sicily, except for a single imperfect example from a small cave on the coast near Syracuse.

There has also recently been found a little stone idol in the Conzo cave, which may be compared with the wellknown, analogous examples from the Iberian peninsula.

12. THE CAMPIGNIAN INDUSTRY IN SICILY AND THE WORKING SITES IN THE HYBLAEAN HILLS

In addition to the worked flakes which are generally used for the smaller and finer implements, a new technique is now widespread in the working of flint, which was usually employed for the making of coarser and bigger implements.

This is the Campignian technique, unknown in the Neo-lithic, but which lasts in Sicily right into the Early Bronze Age. The implements were made from large irregular pieces of flint coarsely flaked on the surface: they have large bulbs of percus-sion and are roughly made into points and discoidal scrapers (especially common at Sant' Ippolito).

As a rule the retouching is on both facets and produces dis-coidal or amygdaloid implements that are somewhat reminiscent of Upper Palaeolithic *coups de poing* and of the Mousterian discoidal cores.

But the most characteristic of all in this industry are the *tranchets*, sometimes of very large size and made into real flint axes.

This Campignian 'core' type of industry generally adopts a material of less good quality than the one used in the blade industry, a whitish opaque flint or even silicious chalk.

This industry was chiefly identified through the work of Ippolito Cafici on the huge 'working floors' in the Hyblaean Hills. A group of these sites extends for about eleven miles over the districts of Vizzini, Licodia Eubea, Monterosso Almo and Giarratana, taking in the localities of San Cono, Fiumegrande, Rubalà, the valleys of the Amerillo and Lavandaio, but espe-cially the Scalona and Calaforno fees, where there are very large exposures of flint strata. The rough-out implements and waste flakes from this flint working are found on the ground here in large quantities.

But the finest and most perfect of these implements generally come from the habitation sites, furnished from these workshops, as those of San Cono, Serraferlicchio, Sant' Ippolito, etc. Some of these working sites, especially Calaforno, produce pebbles of various shapes, ovoid, flattened or rounded with hollows made on the opposite facets, of a type also found sometimes in other countries, associated with the Campignian industrial technique.

13. THE COPPER AGE: CONCLUSIONS

The painted-pottery Neolithic, in spite of the variety of its decorative styles that characterized it from the Castellaro to the Diana phases, represented—in its entirety—a unity. It was easy to recognize the course of its evolution, to follow the progress from one phase to another, and to find precedents in one phase for the stylistic developments of the next.

The Copper Age was also to some extent a unity. This can be well enough shown by the fact that almost all the most important sites continued to develop at least through some of its phases, if not right through the whole of it; e.g. the Chiusazza and Conzo caves, Trefontane, Sant' Ippolito, the Grotta del Vecchiuzzo and Serraferlicchio. But in this case the continuity between one phase and another is much less evident. Each period affirms its own heritage of types and forms, decorative motifs and techniques, and seems wholly to repudiate those of the preceding phases. One has the impression that the world was unstable, in a process of rapid transformation; that these alterations were not caused by any internal evolution based on the continual re-elaboration of those elements that were present, at least in an embryonic state, from the beginning in the patri-mony of these cultures. They took place, it would seem, under the pressure of new influences, new impulses coming from a distant world, and each fresh wave created a new style and taste contrasting rather than in harmony with what had been before.

But it must be admitted that a somewhat similar impression might be gained by anyone who tried to reconstruct Greek civilization, by studying the pottery from only one centre or another in Sicily or Magna Graecia. The contrast between the proto-Corinthian geometric style, the Corinthian with animals, the banded Ionic, and the black or red figure Attic ware, is no less violent than that existing between the various classes of pottery which we have examined.

Like that of the Greeks, the world of the Copper Age, too, must have been both strongly creative and highly diversified. Every region, every ethnic group, must have added its own highly individual and specialized contribution to the rapid progress of an extraordinarily rich and complex civilization.

This particularization was probably in existence already in the Aegeo-Anatolian cultures from which all this complex originated.

Every district in this region, every centre so far excavated, presents at this time its own cultural individuality and its own physiognomy. Although it shares certain elements with neigh-bouring or more distant centres, it is still clearly distinguished from them.

The frequent alternation of the decorative pottery styles in Sicily during the Copper Age can be explained not only by the rapid cultural evolution in the civilization, but still more by the fact that people from different regions and with different heritages were participating in this colonizing movement, or at least in the westward propagation of culture.

We have seen that the first two phases of cultural evolution in the Sicilian Copper Age were still apparently closely linked to the Late Neolithic cultures (Larisa-Rachmani-Eutresis) of continental Greece, and eventually, through these cultures, Anatolian influences reached Sicily.

In the more evolved phases, however, such as those of Malpasso and Sant' Ippolito, the dominant influence was that of the Anatolian Early Bronze Age cultures.

Contributions from other regions such as Malta, Sardinia, and particularly the Iberian peninsula, with which Sicily was now in touch, added to the Sicilian civilization of this time. But a notable part was played by the local cultural substrata on which the new civilization impinged. This is shown most clearly in the case of the incised pottery of San Cono-Conca d'Oro style and that of the painted style of Conzo.

However rapid one may suppose the evolution of any one style to have been, or however short the duration of each, the very number of these changes—at least four—shows that this period must, in its entirety, have lasted a long time.

CHAPTER IV

The Early Bronze Age

IT IS DIFFICULT to recognize any true break between the cultures which we have regarded as being of the Copper Age and those representing the real and proper Bronze Age in Sicily, and it seems that the whole island was not affected to the same extent.

As a matter of fact, a fundamental change had taken place in the middle of the Copper Age at the moment when the influence of Anatolian cultures had gained supremacy over the hitherto prevailing one of the Late Greek Neolithic; it was, however, rather a change of taste and style than any abrupt interruption in the course of civilized life.

The transition from the Copper Age to the Bronze Age can be regarded, to a certain extent, as corresponding to a consolida- tion in the trends which had been prevailing in the last phases of the former period, and to a stabilization of the island cultures.

In south-eastern and southern Sicily the artistic liveliness of the earlier phases was followed by a real cultural Koiné; by a culture artistically very stiff, homogeneous, and conservative, that of Castelluccio.

In the Aeolian Islands the economic decadence which seems to have been characteristic of the Copper Age was followed by the Capo Graziano culture—a period of marked revival. This, though quite different in all its artistic manifestations from that of Castelluccio, showed in some ways the same uniformity, the same stiffness, and the same stylistic immobility during a period which we suppose was fairly long.

It is harder to recognize this break in north-western Sicily, where the Conca d'Oro culture seems to have continued to evolve from the preceding period without apparently any abrupt changes. Perhaps we may find hints of this critical change in

Sicily before the Greeks

1	Calcara	33	Maestro
2	Punta di Peppa	34	Branco Grande
	Maria	35	Piano Resti
3	Capo Graziano	36	Sante Croci
4	Serro dei Cianfi	37	Monte Sallia
5	Castellaro	38	Paraspóla
6	Lipari acropolis	39	Aranci
7	Milazzo	40	Priolo
8	Tindari	41	Sabbuci
9	Longane	42	Gela
10	Naxos	43	Manfria
11	Bronte	44	Lavanca Nera
12	Adrano	45	Monte Bubbonia
13	Biancavilla	46	Valcanonico
14	Paternò	47	Priorato
15	Novalucello	48	Milingiana
16	Catania Barriera	49	Raffe di Milin-
17	Valsavoia		giana
18	Monte San Basile	50	Suor Marchesa
19	Cava Cana	51	Monte Dessueri
	Barbara	52	Naro
20	Cava Secchiera	53	Gibil Gabib
21	Bernardina	54	Sabbuccina
22	Cava Mostrin-	55	Monte Gisira
	giano	56	San Cataldo
23	Proprietà Reale	57	Vassallaggi
24	Grotta Chiusazza	58	Montedoro
25	Grotta Masella	59	Raffe di
26	Licodia Eubea		Mussomeli
27	Giarratana-	60	Monserrato
	Donna Scala	61	Caldare
28	Monte Casale	62	Monteaperto
29	Castelluccio	63	Monte Sara
30	Cugni di	64	Santa Margherita
	Calafarina		Belice
31	Cava Lazzaro	65	Torrebigini
32	Cava d'Ispica	66	Marsala

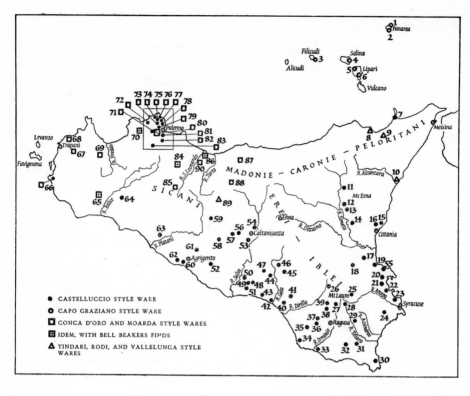

MAP V Early Bronze Age Sites in Sicily

67	Paceco	79	Uditore
68	Erice	80	Boccadifalco
69	Segesta	81	Porrazzi
70	Carini	82	Villagrazia
71	Monte Cuccio	83	Moarda
72	Capaci	84	Villafrati
73	Colli	85	Prizzi
74	Monte Gallo	86	Termini Imerese
75	Valdesi	87	Isnello
76	Mondello	88	Caltavuturo
77	Addaura	89	Vallelunga
78	Leoni	90	Caccamo

the prevalence of western Iberian influences which brought to Sicily the bell-beaker and the decorative style derived from it, and which represented the backwash of the movement of cultural propagation which until now had flowed from east to west.

From the technological point of view the new period is characterized by the prevalence of metal-working, before which the stone industry gradually faded out until it disappeared altogether at the beginning of the Middle Bronze Age.

Politically and economically the Early Bronze Age is marked by another and wider expansion of the civilized world, and by the establishing of lively trade connexions between widely separated countries.

The movement of cultural propagation from the east, which, during the Copper Age, had reached the Iberian peninsula and southern France and inspired in them the splendid cultures of Almeria and Fontbouïsse, did not, however, terminate in those regions. They, in their turn, became cultural centres of impulse and radiated their influence towards more distant lands, towards west-central and northern France and the British Isles.

The first farming cultures to reach these countries were in fact already permeated by evolved cultural elements, such as mega-lithic architecture, the rite of collective burial, and sometimes that of cremation, which clearly show the seed from which they grew—a seed which had fallen on fertile soil. Here also, as had happened in a previous stage on the western coasts of the Mediterranean, prosperous civilizations had been developing, and the exploitation of the natural resources of the soil had been started. Perhaps chief among these was Cornish tin, necessary to the eastern countries for making bronze.

A trade route had gradually been opened, which followed the Atlantic coasts of France, across Aquitaine, and continued along the Tyrrhenian coasts to the Straits of Messina. It carried to the Aegean the tin from the British Isles, for which the refined products of Aegean art and industry were given in exchange. The outcome of this trade was the rise in southern England of the Wessex culture permeated by Aegean influences; but all countries concerned in it felt its beneficial effects.

I. THE EARLY BRONZE AGE IN THE AEOLIAN ISLANDS: THE CAPO GRAZIANO CULTURE

Whereas the Copper Age had been a period of economic decadence in the Aeolian Islands, the Early Bronze Age was a prosperous one. Here the inhabitants availed themselves to the full of their favourable position on the routes which focused on the Straits of Messina from all around the western Mediterranean.

The Aeolian navigators, with many centuries of experience behind them in the export of obsidian, knew by now how to draw the fullest advantages from the new situation that had developed in western Europe. They certainly took a very active part in the trade which linked east and west at this time, and they may even have monopolized it.

Lipari, Filicudi, Salina and Panarea became markets for the trade of the Mediterranean, and perhaps marked the farthest point reached by the Aegean navigators. They exchanged the refined products of their art and craftsmanship there for the raw materials brought from afar by the Aeolian ships.

One clear indication of the exchanges carried out through the agency of the Aeolian Islands lies in the large quantity of Aegean pottery dating from the end of the Middle Helladic and the beginning of the Late Helladic periods, which are found in the Aeolian villages at this time. The amount shows that Aegean products must have been widely diffused in the Aeolian villages.

The Aeolian civilization of this period has been called the Capo Graziano culture, after a village on a promontory of that name in Filicudi.

Plate 32

Capo Graziano is an isolated hill, rising steeply from the sea, and joined to the island by a tongue of low ground. Only on the side facing the isthmus is the slope less steep, and here it is now terraced: on the other sides it is precipitous and in many places completely inaccessible. On the top of this hill the village was built in a very strong, almost impregnable position. Excavations at this site have hardly begun, but have already revealed six oval huts. All that remains today is the surround-

Plate 33

ing dry-stone wall of each hut which once supported a thatched roof. On the southern slope of the hill, in the natural crevices between the huge masses of fallen rocks, the burial places belonging to the people of this village have been found. They seem to have been collective tombs, suggesting an adaptation to the natural conditions of the ground of the ritual type of rock-cut tomb which is now the usual type in Sicily and southern Italy. Here it could not be adopted because of the hardness of the rock.

On the acropolis site in Lipari excavations have also brought to light a village of this period. We have already spoken at length of this acropolis, which, with its isolated position and steep sides, is a natural fortress like the Capo Graziano hill.

The main building of the village is a large oval hut, measuring about forty by twenty-five feet, standing inside a rectangular enclosure. This building may have been the village sanctuary or the dwelling of the chief. Clearly it is markedly different from all the other huts, which are much smaller, not exceeding twenty feet at most, oval in shape, and with only one room: they cluster close together outside the precinct of the biggest hut. A big granary has also been revealed in this village, shaped like a truncated cone, and built most carefully with rubble and volcanic mud.

Other huts of the same date are also being brought to light

in Lipari in an unfortified position in the Diana plain at the foot of the acropolis. This fact shows that at least for some time during this period, which we are inclined to think was rather long, men were able to live free from the anxieties of self-defence. These huts in the Diana plain might be thought to be earlier than those on the acropolis, and to have corresponded to an initial phase of the Capo Graziano culture, before commercial exchanges with the Aegean began. It is a definite fact that no single fragment of Aegean pottery has been found in them, though it is common on the acropolis.

Of a village of this period on the east coast of the island of Salina, at the Serro dei Cianfi near Santa Marina, nothing is left except the refuse which fills a little natural hollow. Its houses, which must once have stood on the top of the hill (Serro), have been washed away by natural agencies. Belonging to the same period, a series of peculiar little pits built of boulders cemented with volcanic mud have been discovered in the Calcara in the island of Panarea. The Calcara is a small scoop, facing the sea, with very steep cliffs and with a little flat area at the bottom, most of which is riddled with active *fumarole* (smoking holes). These are the most salient volcanic phenomena surviving in the island.

This place, difficult of access by foot, was too uncomfortable and too cramped to have been the site of a village; nevertheless, there are indications that the area was frequented from the Late Neolithic (Diana style period) up to Imperial Roman times—a span of nearly two thousand five hundred years. We are led to wonder if we are not here faced with vestiges of a cult devoted to some divinity which presided over the subterranean forces of Nature. If so, the little pits would not have been just granaries, but kinds of *bothroi* for votive offerings.

In the villages of Capo Graziano times, the obsidian industry is relatively rare, though not altogether abandoned. A greenstone axe with cylindrical perforation has been found in Lipari.

Querns are always common, as well as rubbing stones, mortars and pounders. Metal-working on the spot is shown by a sandstone mould for casting bronze objects, found on the Lipari acropolis. The quantities of spindle-whorls, mostly very large in size, prove that the art of spinning and weaving was widespread.

The pottery in the Capo Graziano culture is made of a rather coarse paste, and very often decorated with incised wavy lines, alternating with dotted lines or rosettes, or with little impressed hollows. Dotted triangles are also common. This is a kind of pottery for which we know no parallels, either in Sicily or southern Italy, and which seems therefore to be characteristic only of the Aeolian Islands.

Fig. 18

Actually, some of the forms are similar to those of the earliest Copper Age sites in Apulia, such as those of Gioia del Colle. But the style of decoration is entirely foreign to Apulia. Some vaguely comparable material can be found in Sicily, in the Conca d'Oro culture, which, though earlier in origin than the Aeolian Capo Graziano culture, must have continued to flourish side by side with it.

Evidence of connexions between the two cultures is supplied by typical specimens of Aeolian pottery of the Capo Graziano style which have been found within the area of the Conca d'Oro culture at Villafrati and Moarda; and there is a curious resemblance, not only in the shape of the pots but also in some of the most characteristic decorative motifs of the Capo Graziano culture, with the Maltese pottery of the Tarxien necropolis; belonging, that is, to the period following that characterized by the megalithic buildings in Malta.

Rather than claim direct relationship between the Lipari and Malta cultures, we should perhaps consider them as having been derived from common prototypes, and for these we should logically look towards the East.

In fact, in the Peloponnesus there does exist a class of ware that is very strictly comparable both to the Aeolian and the Maltese pottery. This was found by Dörpfeld in the Altis site at Olympia, where there was a group of tombs with inhuma⁄ tions in large pithoi like the ones we shall later find at Milazzo. At Olympia there were cups that are in every way analogous

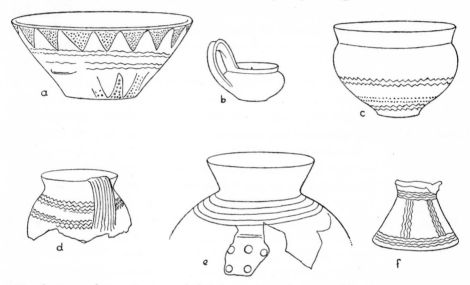

Fig. 18   Pottery of Capo Graziano style from the Lipari acropolis. Height of (f) 2⅜". Lipari Museum.

to our forms, and they also have an identical decoration, continuing, like ours, under the base.

We may also note that pottery forms analogous to those from Capo Graziano are found on many Late proto⁄Helladic and Middle Helladic sites (Eutresis, Orchomenos, Asine, Lerna, etc.). We should therefore also consider an Oriental origin for this Aeolian culture.

The Aeolian culture of Capo Graziano holds a key position in the panorama of Mediterranean prehistory, because it enables us to recognize relations with contemporary cultures of far⁄off lands, and to draw chronological conclusions from them.

We have already mentioned the large number of sherds of imported Aegean pottery that are found in the Aeolian villages and date from this time. The chronology of the Aegean pottery has by now been fairly accurately established.

The discovery of Egyptian objects in the Cretan palaces or on the Greek mainland, and of Aegean objects in Egypt, has, in fact, enabled us to link the artistic and cultural evolution of the Aegean with that of Egypt, which by now had already moved into history.

The Aegean pottery imported into the Aeolian Islands allows us to date the Aeolian cultures, and to establish the first firmly fixed dates in western prehistory. The Aeolian Islands in their turn can provide a basis, hitherto lacking, for dating the cultures in countries still farther west.

The fragments of Aegean pottery found in Lipari, Salina and Filicudi, in the villages of the Capo Graziano culture, come down to the end of the Middle Helladic, but most of them belong to the proto-Mycenaean (L.H. I—II, about 1550–1425 B.C.), to Mycenaean III A1 (about 1425–1400 B.C.) and some perhaps even to the beginning of Mycenaean III A2 (1400–1375 B.C.). They point, therefore, to the existence of lively contacts between the Aegean world and the Aeolian Islands, in the period from the seventeenth to the fifteenth century B.C.

Plate 30

One cannot, however, exclude the possibility that the Capo Graziano culture may have begun earlier, perhaps even in the eighteenth century B.C., because the levels of this culture are very thick and the huts in the villages seem to have been reconstructed many times.

But in Sicily, at Villafrati, typical little vases of the Capo Graziano style have been found associated in a collective tomb with the well-known bell-beaker, itself a representative of a western, Iberian culture, which had widely influenced the whole of western Europe.

2. THE EARLY BRONZE AGE IN SICILY:
THE CASTELLUCCIO CULTURE

Culturally, Sicily seems to have been very unlike the Aeolian Islands at this time. In fact, it did not have a single homo‚ geneous culture, but it had various cultural provinces, each

Fig. 19   Stone tombs at Castelluccio (Noto).

with its own characteristics. The best‚known culture of this period is that of Castelluccio, which, since 1890, was taken by Orsi to represent the first of the four periods into which he divided the prehistory of Sicily.

The Castelluccio culture stretches over the whole south‚east and south of Sicily. But though it may be regarded as being broadly homogeneous, we can recognize from the style of the painted decoration of its pottery two distinct *facies* in it: one in the east, in the districts of Catania, Syracuse, Ragusa and Gela, and the other farther to the west, corresponding roughly to the province of Agrigento.

First let us consider the eastern *facies*. This takes its name from the village of Castelluccio, about fifteen miles from Noto, and has produced one of the biggest collections of material of this period.

The village stood on the top of a rocky spur stretching out from the edge of the high plateau of Akrai towards the south, with deep valleys on each side isolating it and making it easily defensible. No signs of any huts remain, but Orsi discovered the rubbish-tip belonging to them, which was very rich in potsherds. Several hundred rock-tombs can be seen in the soft limestone cliffs of a little side valley (Cava della Signora). At the time of excavation some of these tombs still contained their grave-goods. They are little, oval, oven-shaped rooms, which seldom reach six feet, and are sometimes less than three feet in diameter. Sometimes they have a small anteroom in front. In each one of them were remains of numerous inhumations. The small entrance doorways, generally not more than two and a half to three feet tall, were sometimes closed with simple dry-

Plate 31

Figs. 19, 20

stone walling, and sometimes with stone slabs, some of which were decorated with spiral motifs in relief. These Castelluccio portal slabs are the only examples of prehistoric stone-carving so far known from Sicily. They are vaguely similar to the carvings from the Maltese temples of the Tarxien period which are, however, not only artistically superior to, but also chronologically earlier than, those from Sicily.

Tombs with a rather more complex architecture are rare; amongst these we can mention one which was entered from a

Plate 36

vestibule with four pillars, a type not unique in the architecture of Sicily at this time.

Castelluccio is one of the most interesting, as well as one of the most complete examples of a village of this period, but it was certainly not the only one of its kind. Small, sometimes even much smaller, villages similar to it must have been common throughout eastern Sicily. But generally nothing remains of these except the rock-cut tombs, sometimes isolated, but more often in little groups.

Continuing northwards from Castelluccio, we may mention the small necropolis of the Reale estate near Syracuse, and groups of tombs in the Priolo district (Cava di Mostringiano),

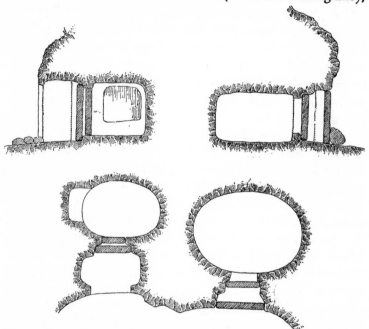

Fig. 20 Plans and sections of the tombs at Castelluccio (Noto). Diameter of large chamber, 30 ft.

at Melilli (Bernadina, Cava Secchiera), at Augusta (Monte Gisira, Cava di Cana Barbára), and the necropolis of Valsavoia on the edge of the Catania plain: all these have oven-shaped tombs. Rather farther inland, however, is Monte San Basile near Scordia, where remains of oval huts have been discovered.

Farther to the north, the Etna lavas were too hard to cut, and so instead of these rock-cut tombs we find various adaptations suited to the local conditions. In the Catania district the hollows formed by the flowing lava were used as ossuaries at Barriera and Novoluccello, but at Biancavilla we find a necro‐polis of oval graves surrounded with little stone walls, and all made inside a big cave formed by the lava flow.

Going southwards from Castelluccio, there are small groups of tombs at Cozzo delle Giumare (Noto), at Cugni di Calafarina (Pachino) and bigger groups in the Cava Lazzaro near Rosolini and in the Cava d'Ispica. In the Cava Lazzaro an extremely interesting tomb has an architectural façade with sham pillars, perhaps the most complex and ornate in Sicily at this time.

Plate 35

Plate 37

On the south coast of Sicily the Comiso district was one of the most densely inhabited during the Castelluccio period. Along the edge of the limestone plateau of Ragusa, and over‐looking the Ippari valley and the plain of Vittoria, a series of villages is strung out, built either on rocky spurs or on little isolated hummocks. The first of these, that of Branco Grande, was built in the sand‐dunes near the Greek town of Camarina. It was fortified with a dry‐stone wall enclosing the oval huts. A short distance away, and farther up the valley, are the villages of Piano Resti, Petraro, Sante Croci and, most important of all, that of Monte Sallia with its cemeteries of Cozzo delle Ciavole and Monte Racello. The prosperity of this village was due to the exploitation of the near‐by flint mines of Monte Tabuto, the abandoned galleries of which were later used as burial places. Out of these came the largest collection of pots of the Castelluccio style ever found. Farther inland are groups of tombs in the districts of Chiaramonte Gulfi (Paraspola, Aranci), of Licodia Euboea, Giarratana (Donna Scala), and the large settlement of Monte Casale between Giarratana and Buscemi, the oval huts of which were discovered by Orsi.

Plate 34

Plate 40

The same cultural *facies* is again found on the other side of the Dirillo river, in the Gela and Caltanisetta districts, at Gela itself (at Molino a Vento, on the Ruggeri estate, in the Borgo tombs), in the tombs of Manfria, and in a number of small cemeteries, most of which are still unexcavated, extending from the borders of the Gela plain (Monte Desusino, Monte Milin-ciana, Priorato, Lavanca Nera, Monte Bubbonia) as far as Caltanisetta (Gibil Gabib, Sabbúcina, San Cataldo, etc.).

The Castelluccio culture is characterized by pottery painted with brown or blackish lines on a light yellow or reddish background, very occasionally with whitish strokes; the forms and decorative motifs are monotonous and frequently repeated. The few forms include: big two-handled amphorae, big basins with a high conical foot, hour-glass-shaped mugs with one or two handles, little low pyxides on a conical foot, small twin vases like salt-cellars, etc. Actually, none of these can be regarded as direct derivatives from the types known from the preceding cultures of Serraferlicchio and Sant' Ippolito.

Plates 28, 29 and 40

The decoration also shows the same uniformity, being based almost exclusively on a motif of crossed bands, or more compli-cated derivatives from it, sometimes looking like chess-boards. As in the preceding cultures, there are many terra-cotta votive horns, weights of various shapes and spindle-whorls. Metal is still rare in the Castelluccio culture, and is generally only repre-sented by some beads and bits of thin copper foil, perhaps used as razors. Two daggers were found at Monte Sallia, and a fragment of a sword from Castelluccio.

The stone industry, on the contrary, is widely diffused, and shows some peculiarities worthy of notice. The predominant industry in these villages is, in fact, a Campignian one, with a rough, sometimes two-sided flaking. In the burial places, on the other hand, blades are often found in large numbers, extremely regular, and sometimes of extraordinary length and perfection, but almost always without secondary working. As always, basalt axes, tiny greenstone axes, often with a perforated butt, querns, rubbers and pounders are common. By this time, too, there are numerous ornaments like beads and pendants made of bone, limestone and other materials.

Like the Aeolian culture of Capo Graziano, the Sicilian Castelluccio culture has revealed elements which enable us to establish links with contemporaneous cultures in other regions. The most important of these consist of some curious elongated bone objects, decorated with a line of bosses with very fine patterns incised on them and on the surrounding field, which Professor John Evans regards as extremely schematized idols. They recur frequently in the tombs of this culture. The necropolis at Castelluccio alone has produced seven of them, some of which, from the fineness of their workmanship and their perfect state of preservation, are the best examples of the series. Other specimens, either whole or fragmentary, have come from the Cava Lazzaro, Sante Croci, Monte Casale, and the Grotta Masella near Buscemi.

The great interest of these objects lies not only in the extremely fine quality of their craftsmanship, which places them amongst the most perfect creations of Sicilian prehistory, but also in the fact that other, almost identical examples have been found outside Sicily. One comes from Malta, another has recently been found at Lerna in the Peloponnesus, in a Middle Helladic level. Three more similar examples, even if less accurately decorated, were amongst material from Troy II–III.

These bossed bone objects provide, therefore, an important chronological link between Sicily, Malta and the Aegean. Actually, the correlations which they suggest are confirmed by several other elements as well.

The Castelluccio painted pottery is a matt-painted ware, certainly closely related, not only by its technique and forms, but also by the style of its decoration, to the characteristic pottery of Middle Helladic times on the Greek mainland. But perhaps even closer similarity can be found with the so-called 'Cappadocian' ware of Central Anatolia (Alishar III, Kültepe, etc.),

Plate 41

which is probably ancestral both to the Greek and the Sicilian variants.

One little vase from Monte Sallia (Tomb I) made of rather different paste from the others in the same cemetery is particularly like the Middle Helladic ones, and Lord William Taylour thinks it may be an imported object. Another tomb at Monte Sallia (Tomb IX) produced a small sword pommel made of bone, analogous to an example from one of the shaft-graves at Mycenae, belonging to the transition between the Middle and Late Helladic. So this definitely would seem to have been an imported object. Lastly, we must remember a small bone plaque from a tomb at Melilli (Cava Secchiera) whose decoration with dotted circles is strongly reminiscent of that of similar bone objects from Troy III, Poliochni V and other Aegean sites.

Plate 29

Plate 43

Plate 42

On the strength of these elements the Castelluccio culture would seem to have synchronized with the Middle Helladic period of the Aegean, or more correctly, perhaps, with the most evolved phases of the Middle and the beginning of the Late Helladic, which would imply an approximate date between 1800 and 1400 B.C. This culture seems, therefore, to have been contemporary with the Aeolian Capo Graziano culture, even if, so far, we have no definite proof of direct relations between the two.

Direct relations do, however, exist between the Castelluccio culture of Sicily and Malta in the period when the splendid local development of megalithic architecture was almost finished there, and later when a cemetery had been made over the ruins of the Tarxien temples.

These Siculo-Maltese connexions are proved not only by the single bossed bone object from Tarxien. Fragments of Maltese pottery of the Tarxien cemetery style have in fact been found in the village of Castelluccio, as well as in one of the Manfria tombs and in the cave of Novoluccello.

3. THE CASTELLUCCIO CULTURE IN THE
AGRIGENTO DISTRICT

A somewhat specialized *facies* of the Castelluccio culture is found in the Agrigento district. In reality we ought rather to speak not only of one but of two distinct *facies*, which, without any doubt, represent two different stages of cultural evolution in this region.

In the first stage we must place the two cemeteries of rock-cut tombs at Naro near Agrigento, and at Partanna near Selinunte. The pots from these necropoleis, both in their forms and in the motifs of their painted decoration, seem to be stylistically closer to the Sant' Ippolito complex, even though in certain respects they resemble Castelluccio types. Thus they seem to belong to pre- or rather perhaps proto-Castelluccio times.

Some of the forms, like the flattened amphorae and the high-necked mugs, can be regarded as slightly modified derivatives from prototypes in the Sant' Ippolito pottery horizon, and they show specially cogent similarities in form with the Conca d'Oro ware, which was strongly influenced by Sant' Ippolito. The prevailing motif in their decoration consists of groups of pendent vertical lines below a horizontal line (which generally emphasizes one of the structural lines in the pot, such as the base of the neck, or the point of the maximum diameter) and stretching down to the bottom, or stopping only a little short of it; a motif which is one of the most typical in the Sant' Ippolito style.

Peculiar to this place, however, and not found at Sant' Ippolito, are the vertical bands of fine cross-hatched lines, and still more the frequent decoration with horizontal bands on the high necks of the pots.

In fact, this style of Naro and Partanna, though still con-nected with forms and decorative elements proper to the Sant' Ippolito *facies*, shows, in comparison with it, some new forms

Fig. 21

and types, and especially a much heavier and more complicated decoration.

Other necropoleis, however, in the same district, such as those of Montedoro, Monteaperto and Monserrato, at a short

Fig. 21   *Painted pottery of the Naro-Partanna style:*
(a) *from Partanna (height about 14");*
(b–e) *from Naro.*
Palermo Museum.

distance from Agrigento, and that of Monte Sara near Cattolica Eraclea, produce pottery in a very different style from that of Naro and Partanna. It is in some ways closer to the East Castelluccio types.

But the decoration is much finer than the Castelluccio one, and covers the whole surface of the pot evenly, though often divided into metope-like panels. The forms, too, are often different; for example, the hour-glass-shaped mug, so common in eastern Sicily, is never found here. What is commonly found instead is a biconical mug on a high foot, which is absent at Castelluccio: this, even more than the East Castelluccio types, is closely comparable to the 'Cappadocian' ware of Central

Plates 38, 39

Plate 39

117

Anatolia. The elements which were reminiscent of Sant' Ippolito in the Naro-Partanna style have almost completely disappeared by now. It seems likely, then, that the culture of Monserrato-Montedoro belongs to a rather later date than that of Naro and Partanna, and therefore to the full prime of the Castelluccio culture.

Two tombs discovered at Torrebigini near Partanna on the extreme western limits of diffusion of this culture are extra-ordinarily interesting for the correlations which they show between the various Sicilian cultures and those of Western Europe at this period. In both these tombs are found fragments of pottery painted in the Monteaperto-Montedoro style, associ-

Plate 23

ated with a ware typical of the Moarda style, as well as some fragments of bell-beakers.

We are here in a border-land between the area of expansion of the western Castelluccio culture and that of the Conca d'Oro. This association of western Castelluccio pottery with that of Moarda seems to point to the contemporaneity of these two cultures, or at least to the survival of the Conca d'Oro culture (which must have had much earlier origins) into the Castelluccio period.

Of even greater importance is the association of both these pottery types with bell-beakers, which confirms in fact the date suggested by the Villafrati tombs, where the bell-beaker was associated instead with pottery of the Capo Graziano style.

Both Villafrati and Torrebigini agree in demonstrating the contemporaneity of bell-beakers with the advanced stages of the Middle Helladic, with which both Capo Graziano and Castelluccio are without any doubt equated.

Since the bell-beakers of Villafrati and Torrebigini belong to a class of ware which was widely diffused over the whole west from the Iberian peninsula to Sicily and Sardinia, northern Italy and southern France and to the Atlantic coast, the Rhine and Danube valleys, and British Isles, the chronological conclusions which we can draw from Sicily will have their repercussions over the whole of Western Europe.

4. THE VALLELUNGA TOMB AND THE EARLY BRONZE AGE IN NORTH-EASTERN SICILY

In the Syracuse Museum there is a group of vases from a tomb accidentally discovered many years ago at Vallelunga, about twenty miles north-west as the crow flies from Caltanisetta.

Its contents included some very large, high-footed, painted basins with rather curious forms, and decorative motifs which must certainly belong to the Castelluccio painted-pottery complex. There are also a series of smaller basins, some high-footed undecorated fruit-stands of types analogous to some from Sant' Ippolito and Moarda, and a number of deep cups with very high handles, sometimes terminating in the shape of an axe, sometimes branching into two tall prolongations in shape like a horse's ears.

Fig. 15, b

Until recently these cups from Vallelunga had no parallels in Sicilian prehistory, but in the last few years fragments of similar handles have been found in various places in the province of Messina: at Tindari, at Longane (Castroreale) and in the area of Greek Naxos near Taormina. At Tindari, in the levels characterized by these types of pottery, fragments of pots in the Aeolian Capo Graziano style were also found, while in the Capo Graziano levels on the Lipari acropolis there was a sherd of a tall-handled dipper of a type known from Tindari and Longane.

One therefore gets a glimpse of a new cultural *facies* in the Sicilian Early Bronze Age, which may stretch along the whole northern coast of the island from Termini Imerese to the Straits of Messina, and about which up to now we know very little. It seems, however, to have been contemporary with the Capo Graziano, Castelluccio and Moarda cultures.

CHAPTER V

The Middle Bronze Age

IN THE MIDDLE BRONZE AGE the conditions of life in the Aeolian Islands and Sicily do not seem to have been very different from those in the preceding period. The villages are in all ways similar and in some cases, as at Filicudi, Lipari, Serro dei Cianfi in Salina, and in the Comiso district, seem to have continued in use from one phase to another.

The tomb types, at least in Sicily, remain identical, and here again there are some necropoleis or burial caves (Catania, Barriera) that continue to be used. Strong connexions still persist with the east, as is shown by the discovery of pottery and other Aegean products.

But side by side with these similarities there are also some noticeable differences. Both in the Aeolian Islands and in Sicily there is a complete change in pottery types between the Early and Middle Bronze Ages, and the change is both too abrupt and too radical to be explained as the result only of taste and fashion. None of the forms or decorative motifs in use in the cultures of Capo Graziano or Castelluccio are found again in the next phase.

The Aeolian culture of Milazzese and the Sicilian one of Thapsos have completely new pottery types, and they have many features in common. Sicily and the Aeolian Islands in this respect seem to have been more closely linked than at any other time in their prehistory since the Diana period, even though there were always very appreciable differences between the two regions as well.

Of all the pottery groups in the preceding phase, the one which presents the closest analogies to the Milazzese and Thapsos cultures is quite clearly that of Vallelunga, Tindari, Longane, not only in the similar quality of its monochrome

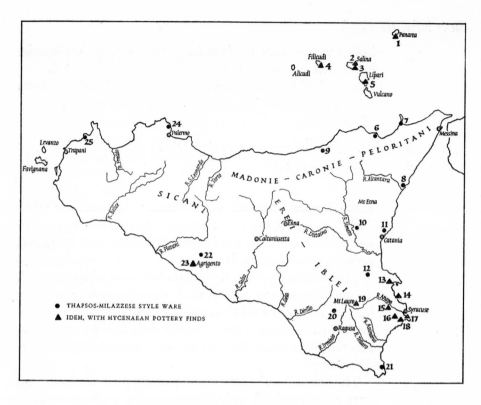

MAP VI Middle Bronze Age Sites in Sicily

1	Milazzese	10	Paternò	18	Matrensa
2	Portella	11	Catania Barriera	19	Buscemi
3	Serro dei Cianfi	12	Lentini	20	Paraspola
4	Capo Graziano	13	Molinello di	21	Grotta Cala-
5	Lipari acropolis		Augusta		farina
6	Tindari	14	Thapsos	22	Caldare
7	Milazzo	15	Floridia	23	Agrigento
8	Naxos	16	Cozzo del	24	Grotta del
9	Grotta di San		Pantano		Ferraro
	Teodoro	17	Plemmyrion	25	Grotta Mangiapane

brown ware, so different from the painted ware of Castelluccio, but also in its pottery forms, and in the types of handles.

In the Middle Bronze Age the north-eastern Sicilian cultures may have prevailed over all the other near-by regions.

I. THE MIDDLE BRONZE AGE IN THE AEOLIAN ISLANDS AND AT MILAZZO

In the Aeolian Islands the Middle Bronze Age culture is called the 'Milazzese culture' after a village excavated on the promontory of that name in the island of Panarea and belonging exclusively to this period.

This village, in which thirty-three huts have been excavated, occupied the top of a narrow, sickle-shaped spur of rock jutting into the sea and joined to the island only by a small saddle of land. It had vertical and inaccessible cliffs, at almost all points, and the site was therefore an excellent natural fortress, easily defensible.

Plate 44

The huts, all oval with the exception of one rectangular one, were often provided with a quadrangular enclosure outside, and were clustered together on the restricted area of the promontory. Some of the huts contained a narrow ledge inside, and some had areas of paved flooring as well as large slabs of stone which might have been used as tables, querns, grain-rubbers and mortars.

Plates 45, 46

Another village of the same period was discovered in the summer of 1955 at Portella, near Santa Marina, on the east coast of the island of Salina. Here, too, the villagers had selected a very strong position: a narrow mountain ridge, dropping steeply from the side of the volcano to the sea. Flanked throughout its length by two deep erosion gullies, with steep walls overlooking them, it stood on cliffs towering very high over the sea. The position was hazardous because of its steepness, and only a serious and imminent danger could have induced people to settle there.

On this slippery slope ten huts were discovered. On the landward side these were partly dug into the ground, and on the seaward side were built in elevation. All were circular and

Plate 47

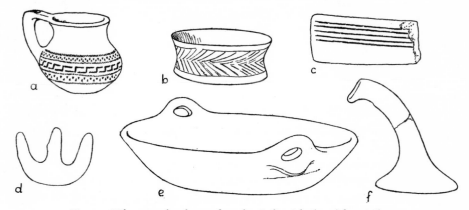

Fig. 22   Milazzese cultural types from the Aeolian Islands and from Milazzo:
    (a) *spout-handled vase from the Milazzo necropolis;*
    (b) *ring-shaped vase support from the Lipari acropolis;*
    (c) *sandstone mould for casting little bronze bracelets, from Milazzese in*
       the island of Panarea;
    (d) *pottery hook from Milazzese on the island of Panarea;*
    (e) *large pan from the above site; diam. $25\frac{1}{8}''$;*
    (f) *votive horn from the Lipari acropolis; height $5\frac{1}{8}''$, others (except (e)) to scale.*
               Lipari Museum.

with only one room. They seem to have been violently destroyed, and in some of them were evident traces of fire; among the household objects covered by their collapse were numerous pots, querns, rubbers and some mortars, as well as some enormous *pithoi* for holding water, a very precious com-modity in such a place.

In the island of Filicudi, the village on the Capo Graziano promontory survived until this time, since its upper levels produced pottery of the Milazzese style. Huts belonging to this

Plates 32, 33

period overlie the earliest ones, and on the Lipari acropolis, too, we find a village, the oval huts of which (sometimes, like those in Panarea, with an adjoining room) overlie the earlier huts of the Capo Graziano period.

No tombs of this period have been found in the Aeolian

Fig. 23   *Apennine pottery from the Italian mainland found in the area of the Aeolian Milazzese culture:*
(a) *from the village of Portella on the island of Salina, diam.* 7½";
(b, c) *from the Milazzo necropolis.*
Lipari Museum.

Islands, but near Milazzo, on the opposite shore in Sicily, a huge necropolis was excavated, which belongs to this same cultural *facies*. It was a necropolis with individual crouched burials, the bodies being contained in huge vases, which are often *pithoi* identical to those from the Salina huts. At other times they are large amphorae with one handle and a cylindrical neck. The cemetery belonged to a settlement on the top of a rocky height which was later the acropolis of Greek Mylai.

Plate 49

We have already said that the pottery of the Milazzese period is very different from that of the Capo Graziano times. It comprises few forms, though very characteristic ones: cups on very high tubular stands, decorated with raised ribs, forming opposing spirals, jars, also decorated with ribs, globular bottles and ring-like vase-supports.

In the necropolis of Milazzo other very interesting forms occur as well: pyxides on a conical foot, and beak-handled vases, both forms of undoubted Aegean-Anatolian origin.

The coarse ware includes big *pithoi*, jars, pans, mugs and little amphorae of various shapes. There are numerous terra-cotta spindle-whorls of various forms, cylindrical, discoid, flattened-biconical, and always of very large size. There are also terra-cotta amulet horns, and simple or double hooks.

The flint and obsidian industry has by now completely disappeared. The use of metal is confirmed by moulds for bronze objects, for swords (Lipari) or for ribbon-bracelets (Panarea).

The villages of the Milazzese period must have had contacts with the peoples of the near-by coasts of the Italian mainland. Certainly they traded with them, even if it was perhaps the danger they feared from the mainland that induced them to settle in uncomfortable but easily defensible sites.

In the Aeolian villages at this time, as well as in the Milazzo tombs, imported pots belonging to the so-called 'Apennine' culture characteristic of the Bronze Age in the Italian mainland were found in association with the local wares. These are very important because they make it possible to synchronize the Aeolian Milazzese culture with a very precise moment in the evolution of the still little known Apennine culture.

Of even greater interest is the discovery in levels of the Milazzese culture, of pottery and other objects imported from the Mycenaean world. This points to the continuation of those

Plate 48
Plate 50
Fig. 22, b

Plate 50
Fig. 22, a
Fig. 25, a, d
Fig. 22, e

Fig. 22, f
Fig. 22, d

Fig. 22, c

Fig. 23

commercial and cultural connexions with the Aegean, of which we had already had proof in the preceding period, and which provides us with a basis for dating this culture.

Whilst the sherds found in the Capo Graziano levels belong to the very end of the Middle Helladic (before 1550 B.C.), to the proto-Mycenaean (L.H. I–II, etc.) and to Mycenaean III A1 (about 1425–1400 B.C.), those found in the villages of Milazzese seem rather to belong to the better known Mycenaean style (L.H. III A, about 1400–1300 B.C.).

It is actually the same pottery as that found in Egypt in the ruins of Tell el Amarna, the capital of Pharaoh Amenophis IV (1372–1355 B.C.).

Only a few sherds belong to the following phase (L.H. III B, about 1300–1225 B.C.). Their scarcity would seem to show that the Milazzese culture came to an end before the end of this phase, probably therefore not later than the middle of the thirteenth century B.C. On the Lipari acropolis a typical little Mycenaean terra-cotta idol was found amongst the pottery.

Fig. 24

In the village of Portella in Salina a long necklace has recently been found made of various kinds of beads. Some of them are of hard stone and others of vitreous paste or faience. These last are most interesting because they belong to a type well known both in Egypt and in the Mycenaean world, and thus closely datable. They recur frequently all over the west of Europe, in Spain (Fuente Alamo), in southern France, in Brittany, and lastly in England in the Wessex culture, so strongly permeated with Mycenaean influences. These faience beads were therefore a very widely exported product from the east into the west of Europe, and they provide us with the means of recognizing the contemporaneity of the various cultures in which they are found.

The discovery at Portella in Salina adds a link to the chain of finds joining the Aegean to England, and shows us the route by which Oriental products were exported to Western Europe.

The deep cultural penetration of the Mycenaean world into the Aeolian Islands is attested to not only by the quantity of imported objects, but also by the recurrence on locally made

Fig. 24   Necklace from hut F in the Portella village on the island of Salina:
(a) in hard stone;
(b, c) in faience or in vitreous paste; (c) 11½" long, others to scale.
Lipari Museum.

pottery of a lot of potters' stamps. Parallels for at least some of these can be found among the signs in the Minoan‑Mycenaean linear script, which are chiefly known from the tablets of the archives in the Minoan palaces of Knossos, Hagia‑Triada and the Mycenaean palace at Pylos amongst others. The use itself of such potters' marks is a Mycenaean one.

These marks are usually put at hidden points on the vases,

Fig. 25

127

below, or on the back of the handles of cups and jars, and inside the circular vase supports, so that it is impossible to think that they were intended for decorative purposes: it is only on the *pithoi* that they are placed very visibly on the shoulder. These marks are almost always single, but occasionally they are in pairs or in groups of three. Some of these marks, consisting of dots, seem to have had a numerical significance, but if so, the system is different from the one used in the Minoan Mycenaean scripts. In some cases the marks are cruciform, and quite often they are associated with single, double or triple impressions of a dotted, hatched or fish scale pattern. In these cases it seems that there is no ground for attributing any literal significance to them. But at other times the graphic character of the marks seems evident, even if they do not have exact parallels in the known signs of the Aegean linear script.

The bold Mycenaean voyages towards the coasts of Sicily and beyond the Straits of Messina, which are attested to by the numerous imported objects, broke off almost entirely in the turbulent period which followed. But they lived for a long time in the memory of the Greek world, and are clearly echoed in the legends handed down to us in the *Odyssey*. Sicily is the country rich in unexploited resources inhabited by the wild Cyclops; the dangers of the straits are adumbrated in the legend of the two monsters Scylla and Charybdis who prevent sailors from crossing over; beyond the straits are the Planctai, the roaming islands whose gloomy heights are always covered with murky cloud, the country of the man eating Lestrigons, the Sirens bewitching the sailors, the island of the enchantress Circe. There is also Aeolia, the floating island surrounded with a bronze wall, ruled by Aeolus, the just and hospitable king, dispenser of the winds, who welcomes Odysseus kindly and gives him the pigskin bag containing a favourable wind for his speedy return home.

2. THE THAPSOS CULTURE IN SICILY

On the east coast of Sicily at this time there was a flourishing culture closely related to that of the Aeolian Islands. This is chiefly known from a group of coastal villages in the country around Syracuse, Plemmyrion, Matrensa, Cozzo del Pantano,

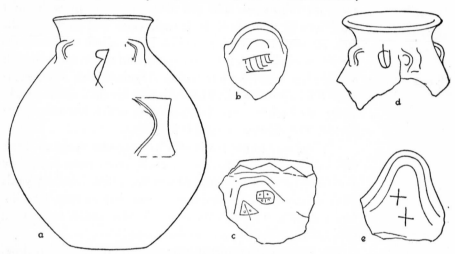

Fig. 25   Pots of the Aeolian culture of Milazzese with incised potters' marks:
(a, c) from the Lipari acropolis, height of pot $23\frac{5}{8}''$;
(b, d, e) from Milazzese on the island of Panarea.
Lipari Museum.

Floridia, Thapsos and Molinello of Augusta. Of the villages themselves scarcely anything remains, except the necropoleis with rock-cut oven-tombs dug into the soft limestone. The excavation of these tombs by Orsi has enriched the Syracuse Museum with an outstanding collection of finds.

The most important of these villages is Thapsos, which occupied the present peninsula of Magnisi, between Syracuse and Augusta; here on the sea-shore are remains of some hundreds of rock-tombs as well as some smaller groups in the interior of the peninsula. The tombs are of two types. Those on the plateau are reached by a vertical shaft always provided with a step to facilitate access to the funeral chamber; those on the coastal cliff open straight on to the outside with their small doors. Because the slope is so gradual, some of the little chambers had a very long channel cut in front of them to drain

Plate 51

away the rain-water. The chambers are generally wider and more regular than those at Castelluccio, and in their walls there are often one or more niches. In some loftier tombs there is a whole circle of niches in the walls, and the doorway to each

Plate 52

of these has a crescent-like frame. Another tomb when exca-vated still had an antechamber with pilasters cut in the live rock, on top of which was a roof of large slabs which has now disap-peared. The doorway into the chamber was framed in relief.

A short way to the north of Thapsos, near Augusta, there was a little village on the top of a rocky promontory formed by a narrow bend of the river Molinello, a few hundred yards from its mouth. The tombs, no more than twenty, opening into the cliffs, were like those at Thapsos, much larger than those of Castelluccio, and tholos-shaped.

The Plemmyrion cemetery is on the promontory which closes the Great Harbour of Syracuse on the south: here the tombs are all of the type with a little shaft, but some of them have a small antechamber between this and the funeral chamber, in which the numerous niches often have a crescent-like frame, similar to the Thapsos ones.

The Cozzo del Pantano village was on the top of an isolated knoll, rising in the plain near the source of the Kyane river, about three miles to the south of Syracuse. The corresponding tombs, about sixty in number, are dug out on the north and south slopes of the knoll, either singly or in little clusters. Some of them have an open forecourt with an antechamber: nearly all of them have side niches.

Between Plemmyrion and Cozzo del Pantano, in the plain by the Torre di Milocca, is the little group of tombs of Matrensa, most important not only for its being one of the first to be excavated in Sicily, but also for the richness of the pottery and Mycenaean vases recovered from one of the tombs.

Plate 59

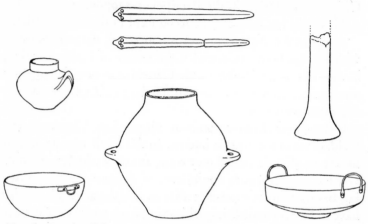

Fig. 26   Grave-goods from a tomb on Monte San Vincenzo near Caldare (Agrigento). Height of large pot 14⅛", others to scale. Syracuse Museum.

A layer containing pottery of the Thapsos style has recently been discovered in the Chiusazza cave, still in the Syracuse neighbourhood. An isolated find comes from a tomb acciden-tally discovered in the Maiorana neighbourhood near Buscemi on the Monte Lauro plateau.

Farther to the north of the group of necropoleis just described, traces of the same cultural *facies* were found at Lentini where some vases of Thapsos style were discovered.

An outstanding group of pottery in this style comes from the Barriera caves on the outskirts of Catania, and some vases from Nizeti in the same district should also be mentioned. Another group comes from the acropolis of Paternò on the slopes of Etna. A layer of the Thapsos period has recently been identified on the site of the Greek Naxos (Taormina).

To the south of Syracuse and along the southern coast of Sicily traces of this culture are so far fewer. Nevertheless, some groups of vases show that the villages in the Comiso district must in some cases at least have survived up to this time. Some tombs with pottery of Thapsos style have been found at Chiaramonte Gulfi, in the Paraspola necropolis.

This *facies* has not yet been recognized in the Gela district.

As far as the Agrigento area is concerned, the only place in which it has been discovered is the village of Caldare which, having flourished chiefly in the Castelluccio period, lasted on till this time; for to it must be attributed typical high-footed cups decorated with ribs.

Fig. 26
Grave-goods from a tomb at Monte San Vincenzo near Caldare are of the greatest interest. In this tomb were associated some pots of undecorated grey ware, amongst which were some very tall tubular stands reminiscent of Thapsos types; also two big basins of sheet bronze as well as two daggers. The basins have so far no parallels in prehistoric Sicily, and they may have been imports from the Mycenaean world; the daggers, as a matter of fact, are more like those which we shall find in the immediately following period at Pantalica and Dessueri than those from Thapsos and analogous sites. The Caldare tomb could therefore be attributed to the very end of the Middle Bronze Age. From outside Agrigento there comes a little Mycenaean jar, which should also be referred to this phase.

The only elements presumably belonging to this time from the extreme west of Sicily are a few sherds of decorated ribbed cups found in the upper levels of the Mangiapane cave near Custonaci in the province of Trapani.

Fig. 27, e
The pottery of the Thapsos culture has very close analogies with that of the Aeolian Milazzese culture. Some of the forms, as for example the cups on high tubular stands and some of the techniques and decorative motifs, are absolutely identical.

Others are markedly different. In the Syracuse neighbourhood there is, however, a greater variety of forms and motifs than in the Aeolian Islands. Common here, for instance, are the huge carinated basins on very high tubular stands and with slightly bifurcated handles, some little bowls on very high tubular stands, in one case having a smaller bowl standing within it.

Fig. 27, a

Fig. 27, d

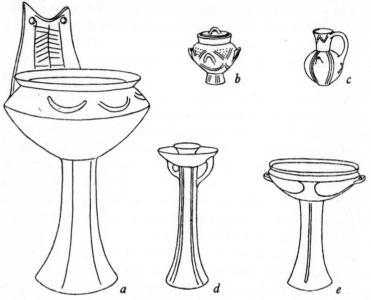

Fig. 27   Pottery forms of the Thapsos culture:
(a–c and e) from Thapsos; (d) from Matrensa. Height of (a) 24″, others to scale.
Syracuse Museum

(This was possibly for use as a lamp; if so, it might be a poor imitation of the steatite 'lamps' from the Minoan palaces.) The one-handled bottles have more varied forms than in the Aeolian Islands, and, as well as the heart-shaped or globular pyxides on a foot, there are others without feet or cylindrical in shape. The little jars and dippers are in great variety, and these always have very high handles, often bifurcated at the tip, and therefore heralding the horned type of handle. Spout-handled vases are also found here.

Found with this indigenous pottery in the Syracusan villages of this period is a kind of pottery with simpler shapes, decorated exclusively with horizontal bands of incised grooves a little below the rim, which can technically and stylistically be identified with the Maltese pottery of Borg-in-Nadur: these include some bottles and deep truncated conical cups, either footless or provided with a high conical foot.

While the Aeolian *facies* of Milazzese is closely linked with the Italian mainland, the Syracusan Thapsos culture seems to be connected rather with Malta. But here, too, as in the Aeolian Islands, there are evident proofs of intensive commercial contacts with the Aegean world. The tombs of this period at Thapsos, Cozzo del Pantano, Matrensa, Floridia, Buscemi and Molinello of Augusta have produced a quantity of Mycenaean pots, some of which are very fine. One of the earliest pieces is perhaps an alabastron recently discovered at Thapsos, dating back to the beginning of Mycenaean III A, i.e. to the end of the fifteenth century B.C. So far it is the only one of its kind in Sicily. The other pieces almost all belong, however, to the more advanced or final stages of the same period, spaced throughout the fourteenth century B.C. Most of them are small pithoid jars, and two specimens from

Plate 59

the Matrensa tomb should specially be mentioned for their decoration and their perfect state of preservation. An odd specimen also comes from Agrigento. A cup from Cozzo del Pantano in the Ephyrean style is perhaps the most artistically outstanding piece of the series. The latest specimen is a false-necked jar from the Maiorana locality near Buscemi, attributable to Mycenaean III B, and therefore within the thirteenth century B.C.

In the Plemmyrion tombs there were found two necklaces of

Plate 55

faience beads analogous to those from Salina, and an ivory

comb decorated with spirals, also certainly an eastern import. No potters' marks have so far been found in vases in Sicily.

In these Syracusan tombs bronze weapons and implements begin to appear fairly frequently, and their types show their evident Mycenaean derivation. The most important item among the weapons is the great Plemmyrion sword which is akin in type to most of the short swords and daggers from the other Syracusan necropoleis, while the two bigger daggers from the

Fig. 28 Pottery of the Maltese Borg'in'Nadur style from the Cozzo del Pantano necropolis (Syracuse).
Height of left-hand object 15″, other to scale.
Syracuse Museum.

Caldare tomb with their broader blades and rounder tips are more reminiscent of the types which we shall find in the necropoleis of the following period at Pantalica, Caltagirone and Dessueri.

Ornaments are few. They include some ribbed ribbon brace-lets like those which must have been cast in the mould found in Panarea. A fragment of a vase made of sheet bronze joined with small rivets from the Thapsos necropolis can best be compared with the big basins from Caldare.

Fig. 26

CHAPTER VI

The Late Bronze and the Iron Age

THE PROSPEROUS CIVILIZATION which Sicily and the Aeolian Islands had enjoyed during the Early and Middle Bronze Ages came to an abrupt end about the middle of the thirteenth century B.C.

The peaceful relations and commercial exchanges which had existed between the various Mediterranean peoples were now broken off almost entirely. A time of war and fear began, forcing the peoples to change their whole way of life, and profoundly altering the basis of their economy. A real Dark Age set in, only to be brought to an end five centuries later with the Greek colonization of Sicily and southern Italy.

In the Early Bronze Age, just as in the Copper Age, it does not seem as if any serious danger threatened the Aeolian and Sicilian peoples. The villagers of this period do not seem to have been particularly concerned with defending themselves. The habitation site at Lipari extended into the Diana plain below, as well as being on the acropolis itself.

But by the Middle Bronze Age the danger must have become both more serious and more imminent, and must have been felt much more acutely in the Aeolian Islands than in Sicily. This menace came from the coasts of the Italian mainland. Only a grave fear could have caused the villages to be placed in such inconvenient situations as those of Milazzese in Panarea and Portella in Salina; this danger proved in the long run to be overwhelming. The old culture was swept away by the incur‹ sions of new peoples, who, arriving from the sea or from across the Straits of Messina, invaded the Aeolian Islands and Sicily.

By now we are at the dawn of protohistory, and even if the facts of this period are not actually written down in a historical document, they are at least strongly echoed by the legends. We can therefore give a name to these new-comers: they are the Ausonians, the Sikels and the Morgetes.

I. THE AUSONIAN CULTURE IN THE AEOLIAN ISLANDS

Diodorus Siculus (*V, 7*) tells us that at first the Aeolian Islands were uninhabited, but that later Liparos, son of Auson the king of the Ausonians, a people of central-south Italy, fell into discord with his brothers. Taking command of an army and some ships, he set out from Italy and occupied the island which takes its name from him, and founded a town there.

In reality the Aeolian Islands were not uninhabited: on the contrary, a civilization at least two thousand years old was flourishing there. But the colonization of the islands by a people coming from the Italian mainland—in other words, the Ausonians of Diodorus' legend—is confirmed by archaeological data.

On the Lipari acropolis, overlying the ruins of the Middle Bronze Age huts destroyed by fire, there is a layer whose extremely characteristic pottery differs completely from that of the preceding period. It has, on the other hand, no counterpart in Sicily. Evidently the cultural unity which existed between the Aeolian Islands and Sicily had been broken.

The material from this layer is strongly related to that from a late phase in the Apennine culture of the Italian peninsula, and more particularly to that from the Apulian villages of Scoglio del Tonno near Taranto, Porto Perone near Leporano and Coppa Nevigata near Manfredonia. This typological identity proves that the Aeolian Islands now suddenly and fully come into the orbit of those Italian cultures with which they had already actively traded in the preceding period. The agreement between the legend and the results of archaeological research could not be closer. Using the evidence of Diodorus,

137

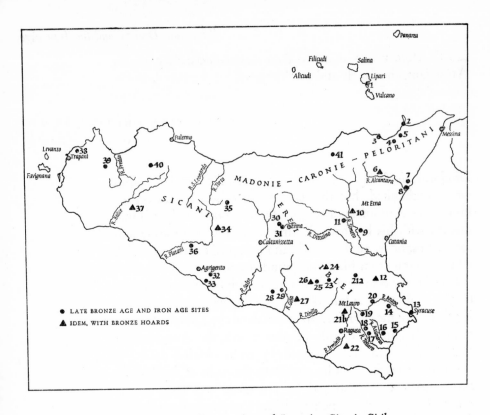

MAP VII Late Bronze Age and Iron Age Sites in Sicily

1	Lipari acropolis	12	Lentini	23	Molino Badia	34	Polizzello

1   Lipari acropolis
2   Milazzo
3   Tindari
4   Longane
5   Pozzo di Gotto
6   Malvagna
7   Cocolonnazzo di Mola
8   Naxos
9   Paternò
10 Mendolito
11 Centuripe

12 Lentini
13 Ortigia
14 Rivettazzo
15 Cassibile
16 Noto Vecchio
17 Finocchito
18 Tremenzano
19 Palazzolo
20 Pantalica
21a Vizzini
21b Giarratana
22 Modica

23 Molino Badia
24 San Cataldo
25 Caltagirone
26 Monte San Mauro
27 Niscemi
28 Butera
29 Monte Dessueri
30 Realmese
31 Calcarella
32 Favara
33 Cannatello

34 Polizzello
35 Valledolmo
36 Sant' Angelo Muxaro
37 Santa Margherita Belice
38 Erice
39 Segesta
40 San Giuseppe Iato
41 Monte Scurzi

we can therefore call the civilization now beginning in the Aeolian Islands the Ausonian culture. An examination of the archaeological material enables us to distinguish clearly two phases in the long evolution of this culture: so we will call these phases Ausonian I and II.

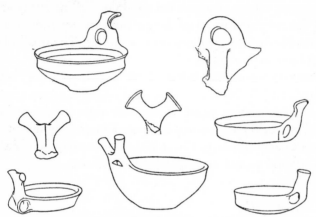

Fig. 29. Ausonian I pottery from the Lipari acropolis. Lipari Museum. Diam. of biggest bowl 8½", others to scale.

(a) Ausonian I

The most obvious feature in the pottery of the first phase of the Ausonian culture is the quantity and variety of terminals or projections on the handles of carinated bowls and small pans, always blackish in colour. These projections are shaped either like a simple cylinder or else like an axe, or there may be two cylinders or a pair of horns branching out from a vertical handle. Or again, the handle may consist of a wide pierced plate topped with opposed volutes. Even the little cordoned handles that rise from the rim of the small dippers have horned terminals.

Fig. 29

The commonest domestic pots at this time are the big cylindrical situlae decorated with a rough cordon and with four little tongues around the rim.

Fig. 30, 1

139

Hitherto this culture has only been found on the Lipari acropolis, where the invaders perhaps settled after having driven out the earlier inhabitants. No signs of it have been found in the smaller islands. The villages of the Milazzese culture in Panarea, Salina and Filicudi were destroyed with violence and were never rebuilt. Perhaps the conditions of insecurity at sea, and the continual threat of danger from enemy raids, made it impossible for small communities to survive. The small islands must have been abandoned.

Some traces of this culture have also been recognized at Milazzo and Tyndaris. At Lipari the level corresponding to this first Ausonian phase is not very thick: the remains of buildings belonging to this time are almost insignificant and its tombs are unknown. One has the impression, therefore, that this cultural period may have been very short.

(b) Ausonian II

Overlying the levels of the first phase of Ausonian culture, there are levels of much greater thickness and richness, the material from which, though differing noticeably from those of the immediately underlying levels, are in some respects un-deniably analogous with them. Evidently one is passing from one cultural phase to another. But there is no impression of any break, or any radical change of culture, such as that between the Milazzese culture and Ausonian I: on the contrary, there is an evident continuity between the two periods. Certainly many of the types characteristic of Ausonian I fall into disuse, and a number of new types and forms now begin to be current.

One notices the absence of many of the most characteristic projections on the handles, and only the horn-shaped one survives, which is now always like a real ox-face, and a new type of raised handle becomes common, the one shaped like a small horizontally fluted column. Together with the cordoned

Fig. 30, c

Fig. 30, a

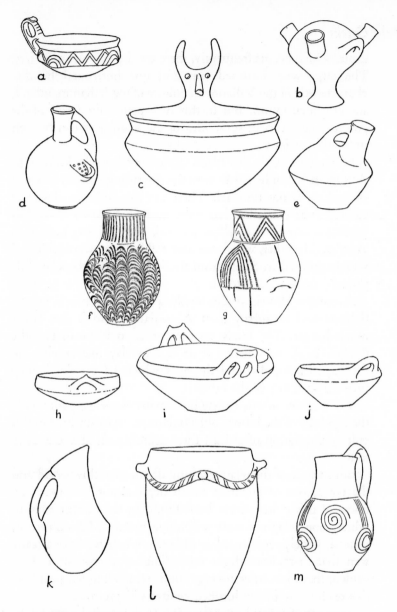

Fig. 30   Ausonian II pottery from the Lipari acropolis. Lipari Museum.
Height of (b) $6\frac{3}{4}''$ (a, c, d, e to scale); (f), (g) $16''$; (l) $15\frac{3}{8}''$ (h–k, m to scale).

Fig. 30, l, f, g situla, which occurs frequently, there are also big biconical jars. The cups with inturned rim and one horizontal handle, *Fig. 30*, h–j characteristic of the Villanovan culture of the Italian mainland, are also often found. But in this new period the forms of the pots are more varied; some idea of the main ones can be seen *Fig. 30* in the illustrations.

In contrast with the black almost exclusively known in Ausonian I, bright red is now the prevailing colour; grooved *Fig. 30*, a, m decoration is not unusual. There are two different classes of painted pottery: the first has a decoration of brown or reddish *Fig. 30*, g geometric motifs on a yellow ground, and is chiefly known in *Fig. 30*, f Apulia. The other, which we may call 'plumed ware', is found widely diffused in Sicily from the beginning of the Cassibile period (about 1000–850 B.C.).

Ausonian II was undoubtedly a period of much greater richness and prosperity than Ausonian I, and it also lasted much longer. The levels corresponding to it are in fact the thickest of all the cultural strata that overlay one another on the Lipari acropolis, and the ones which have yielded more material than any of the others.

We shall see in due course how many elements, particularly the typology of the bronze objects, compel us to attribute to this culture a duration of at least three centuries, from about 1150 to 850 B.C.

But in spite of the relatively long duration of this period and the conditions of apparent prosperity existing in Lipari, no traces of this culture have been found in the smaller islands, which one imagines were still unoccupied. This culture is, instead, widely represented at Milazzo, where we have already seen that there were slight indications of Ausonian I. It is evident that those insecure conditions which had led people to live exclusively in big fortified centres still prevailed.

Remains of many huts belonging to this period were found in the habitation site on the Lipari acropolis; they were all badly damaged by the foundations of Greek, Roman and medieval houses. But enough remained to show that these huts, half cut into the ground, and largely built of wood, belonged to a type known during the Iron Age in central Italy (the Palatine at Rome). We shall see better preserved examples at Lentini in Sicily.

These were no longer round houses like those of the Early and Middle Bronze Ages; they were much bigger buildings, sometimes perhaps rectangular, but in other cases certainly irregularly polygonal. Their floors, paved with stones or gravel, and covered with a layer of clay, were much lower than the ground outside, and the low dry-stone revetment wall around them always preserved the casts of the upright wooden posts which must have been the framework of the hut. Inside, there was always a hearth.

The village on the Lipari acropolis underwent violent destruction. In all the huts a very conspicuous deposit of burnt material was discovered, including all the household goods buried when the huts collapsed. Some of them contained an enormous mass of broken pottery: from one single hut nearly two hundred pots could be reconstructed.

The necropolis belonging to Ausonian times has also been found at Lipari, at the foot of the acropolis, underneath the area of the modern town. A trench which was dug here revealed about fifty tombs; some of them, which were deeper and therefore a little older, were of the type with crouched skeletons placed in big jars, like those of the Middle Bronze Age found at Milazzo. The others, overlying the earlier ones, were cremation burials with the ashes collected in cordoned situlae, laid horizontally in the ground with their mouths closed by large stone slabs. Some of the earlier tombs (those with inhumations in jars) had very rich grave-goods, including gold wire bracelets, necklaces made of amber and vitreous paste, and many bronze objects such as fibulae, little knives, belt-clasps, rings, large pins, etc.

Plate 53

These bronzes, though completely foreign to Sicily, are, however, known on the Italian peninsula. Parallel forms come from the 'terramare' of the Po valley, from the Peschiera lake-village on Lake Garda, from the earliest cremation cemeteries on the mainland, from the hoard of Coste del Marano near Tolfa, and from the Torre Castelluccia village near Taranto.

These comparisons with the Italian mainland show, more-over, that we are still in a relatively early period, and that these Lipari tombs should not be dated later than the twelfth or the first half of the eleventh century B.C. Among the bronzes from the huts on the acropolis some are very ancient, like those from the tombs, while others are of much more recent types, which do not appear in Sicily before the tenth or ninth century B.C. It is just these more recent bronzes that prevent us from dating the Lipari destruction before the middle, or better, perhaps, before the end, of the ninth century.

After the destruction the village does not seem to have been rebuilt. During the period following this destruction, and before the foundation of Greek Lipari by a group of Cnidians and Rhodians in about 580 B.C.—in fact, for two and a half centuries—the Lipari acropolis seems to have been unoccupied. This coincides perfectly with the information we are given from historical sources.

Diodorus Siculus, who is always our authority for these earlier stages of protohistory in the Aeolian Islands, tells us that when the Cnidians arrived in Lipari they found the islands almost uninhabited. There were only five hundred inhabitants who claimed that they were descended from Aeolus. They lived in perpetual fear of raids from the Tyrrhenian pirates with whom the Greeks had immediately to fight.

Nothing remains of the Ausonian village at Milazzo, but a few fragments of pottery show that it must, once again, have been on the castle site, later to be the acropolis of Greek and Roman Mylai. The necropolis of this period was, however,

found at Milazzo, and it differed somewhat from the Lipari
one in having only cremation tombs, with the ashes collected
not in situlae, but in urns covered with a bowl; it stood upright
in a little round hole in the ground, surrounded with slabs or
small stones. It was, in fact, a real 'urnfield' like those which
from this time onwards were to become the commonest type
of necropolis not only in the Italian peninsula, but also in
the whole of Central and Western Europe, from the Danube
valley to the Iberian peninsula. The profound difference between the Lipari necropolis and that of Milazzo is due probably
to a difference in date: the latter, in all probability, coming into
use when the former was finishing. While the Lipari necropolis may roughly be dated between 1150 and 1050 B.C., the
Milazzo one was more likely to have been in use between about
1050 and 850, or 800 B.C.

Plate 54

Both the bowls covering the urns, and the little accompany-
ing pots, are well-known types in the Ausonian II levels at
Lipari; the urns, however, are never found there. We must
assume that they were ritual vases for an exclusively funerary
use, and therefore without any place amongst domestic
belongings.

Though some of the pottery and bronze types from the
Ausonian II villages or necropoleis at Lipari and Milazzo have
parallels in Sicily, most of them are absolutely foreign types,
more closely related to those of the Italian mainland than to
Sicilian ones. The cremation rite, in particular, is totally unknown in Sicily during the Bronze and Early Iron Ages. The
Lipari tombs with situlae for the ashes find their closest
parallels from Torre Castelluccia near Taranto, and the bronze
types from the two sites are also in every way similar.

On the other hand, the Milazzo necropolis, not only in its
tomb types, but also in the shapes and decorations of the urns
and its bronze objects, is strictly analogous with the proto-
Villanovan necropoleis of the Italian mainland, i.e. to those at

Timmari (Matera), Tolfa and Allumiere (Civitavecchia), Ponte San Pietro (Viterbo), Sticciano (Grosseto), Pianello di Genga (Ancona), Bismantova (Reggio Emilia) and Fontanella di Casalromano (Mantua).

The comparisons we can make between the village of this period in Lipari and that of Torre Castelluccia at Pulsano near Taranto are particularly interesting. Not only was the pottery from the two habitation sites identical, but the tombs and grave-goods were also similar. But at Torre Castelluccia, in the levels corresponding to those of Ausonian II in Lipari, there were also many sherds of imported sub-Mycenaean pottery (L.H. III C), showing that a lively trade was still being carried on with Greece at this time. At Lipari were found only two fragments, both from the same crater, stylistically transitional between the sub-Mycenaean and the protogeometric, and though these unfortunately came from disturbed soil, they must surely belong to the levels of this period, and provide the only hint of contacts with the East.

These links with the Aegean confirm the rather high dating for the beginning of Ausonian II (which we had already been led to adopt from the typology of the bronzes in the Lipari necropolis), and the short duration of Ausonian I. We shall not be far from the truth if we assume that Ausonian II was already in existence by about 1150 B.C.

If we can attribute the destruction of the Lipari village to about the middle of the ninth century B.C., Ausonian II must have lasted for at least three centuries.

There is also undoubtedly a strong likeness between the Ausonian II material from Lipari and that from the huts on the Palatine and the earliest tombs in the necropolis of the Forum at Rome. But this likeness is far less strong than that between Lipari and Torre Castelluccia. The discoveries at the Forum and the Palatine belong, in fact, to a rather later time than those of Ausonian II in Lipari, and they might be regarded as types representing a hypothetical Ausonian III which has never been found at Lipari, since it would equate with that period when the acropolis was uninhabited. When the earliest settlement, from which Rome was to develop, was coming into being on the banks of the Tiber, a very old and notable civilization at Lipari, more than twenty centuries old, was coming to its end.

2. SICILY AND THE PROBLEM OF THE SIKELS

The Greeks knew the Sikels as a people who had been living on the Italian mainland at the dawn of protohistory, but who had later been driven into Sicily by other peoples. Though they agree on the general outline, the various Greek historians not only give us different versions of this event, but also different dates.

Thucydides says that the Sikels, driven into Sicily by the Opicians, drove the Sikans towards the south and west of the island about three hundred years before the Greek colonization, i.e. about 1030 B.C. Hellanicus of Mytilene would place this event much earlier: three generations before the Trojan War, in the twenty-sixth year of Alcyon's priesthood at Argos. By using the traditional date of 1180 B.C. for the fall of Troy, and allowing about thirty years for each of the three generations, we arrive at an approximate date of 1270 B.C., almost the same as that (eighty years before the Trojan War) suggested by Philistus of Syracuse.

The Sikels should have brought with them, therefore, a culture of 'late Apennine' type, somewhat similar, at least in its material aspects, to the Ausonian culture at Lipari, to whose inhabitants they must have been closely related. We should consequently expect to find evidence of these people in Sicily from pottery and bronzes of markedly mainland types, and from urnfields like those at Lipari and Milazzo. But we find that the cultural panorama of Sicily in the Late Bronze Age and Early Iron Age was, in fact, very different from what the historical sources lead us to expect, and connexions with the mainland of Italy were either extremely rare or altogether missing.

Paolo Orsi, the first great discoverer of Sicilian prehistory, had, somewhat curiously, called by the name Sikels all the peoples living in eastern Sicily in the Bronze Age, from the time of the Castelluccio culture onwards. He had subdivided all the following prehistoric and protohistoric evolution in Sicily into his four 'Siculan' periods.

This ethnical identification of the Sicilian Bronze and Early Iron Age peoples with the legendary Sikels was very favourably received, and for a long time it was not seriously challenged. And yet to call the Castelluccio and Thapsos cultures 'Siculan' is in complete disagreement with all the dates suggested by the literary sources and historical traditions of the Greek world.

In fact, these two cultures have no affinities with those of the Italian peninsula; on the contrary, they were, as we have seen, permeated with Aegeo-Anatolian elements which would speak in favour of their Oriental origin. Moreover, they were flourish-ing long before the time when the Sikels are supposed to have crossed into Sicily.

The bearers of the Castelluccio and Thapsos cultures were certainly not Sikels. But can we attribute to these people the Pantalica-Cassibile-Finocchito culture which flourished in eastern Sicily after the end of the Thapsos culture? We will try to answer this question by examining that culture.

There is no doubt that the Greeks called Sikels all those indigenous peoples with whom they came in contact when they were founding their colonies on the coast of eastern Sicily in the last third of the eighth century B.C. But the disagreement which exists between the material aspect of their culture as re-vealed by archaeology, and that which historical sources suggest, makes us wonder whether this name really corresponds to any ethnical or historical truth.

3. THE PANTALICA CULTURE AND ITS EVOLUTION

The basic change in the social organization which we have noticed in the Aeolian Islands between the Middle and Late Bronze Ages is again found on a much larger scale and much more clearly in Sicily. Here again we find similar phenomena, doubtless resulting from the same causes.

The numerous little villages of the Thapsos culture scattered along the coast, in positions generally not chosen for defence, suddenly disappear.

To judge from the Mycenaean pottery found in their necropoleis one might suppose that their disappearance took place during the course of the thirteenth century B.C. The inhabitants, abandoning the coastal plains, took refuge in the least accessible hill-country, often extremely hard to live in, regardless of any economic considerations, but with an eye only to their defensive possibilities. They settled in a few big urban centres such as those connected with the huge necropoleis of chamber-tombs at Pantalica, Cassibile, Dessueri, etc.; centres which enabled them to raise an army large enough to resist the onslaughts of a well-armed and warlike foe. Evidently life in this dark age was dominated by fear.

One might well suppose that this lack of security, this threat which hung over the population, and which is reflected in the position of the towns themselves, must be connected with the raids of those barbarous peoples, memories of whom were still alive in Greek times: Sikels, Ausonians, Morgetes, various groups of one ethnical stock who had formerly lived in the Italian peninsula.

The results of archaeological inquiry agree therefore with the traditional historical data, and substantiate Hellanicus' claim for the thirteenth century as the date for this migration: the earliest date among those suggested by the ancient historians.

The conditions of life which obtained in Sicily at this time lasted for a very long while, and in eastern Sicily were still fundamentally unaltered among the indigenous peoples when the Greeks founded their first colonies in the last third of the eighth century. No doubt during this long lapse of over five centuries (about 1250–730 B.C.) the island culture could not have remained at a standstill. Archaeological investigation allows us, in fact, to recognize an internal evolution in this culture, an evolution which is reflected particularly in the changes of the form and decorative style of the pottery, and in the types of weapons and bronze implements.

Before going on to examine the individual archaeological centres in Sicily at this time, let us try to describe the main outlines of this evolution. It is a task made easier for us in southeast Sicily, especially between Syracuse and Gela, where the patient and systematic researches of Paolo Orsi at Pantalica, Cassibile, Finocchito, Syracuse itself, Caltagirone and Dessueri have led to the discovery of much more abundant material than anywhere else.

In the cultural evolution of this district we can clearly recognize four distinct phases between the middle of the thirteenth and the end of the eighth century B.C., each of which has its own characteristics; but we cannot discount the possibility that further research may one day allow us to deal with the matter in even greater and more precise detail.

Let us note, meanwhile, a fact of fundamental importance: throughout this long period the tombs continue to be of the chamber type, proper to the preceding periods, with little ovenshaped rooms cut in the rock. But the concentration of the population in large urban centres resulted in the necropoleis of this age being very much larger and more conspicuous than the Early and Middle Bronze Age ones. In contrast to the few dozens, or at most the hundred tombs of the necropoleis of Castelluccio, Thapsos, Plemmyrion, etc., we now have the thousands of tombs at Pantalica, Cassibile, the Montagna di Caltagirone and Dessueri.

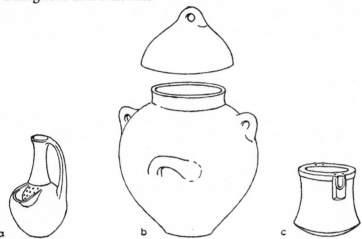

Fig. 31   Glossy-red ware from the Caltagirone necropolis. Height of (b), excluding lid, 10½", others to scale. Syracuse Museum.

Phase I (about 1250–1000 B.C.). This phase is known, above all, from the north and north-western necropoleis at Pantalica, the one of the Montagna di Caltagirone, and from a group of tombs at Dessueri. Characteristic of it is a very beautiful red glossy ware, often including tall tubular stands still in the Thapsos tradition, but by now having substantially different forms, while the quality of the pottery itself has also changed, and it is now certainly wheel-turned. Among the most typical forms at Pantalica are the heart-shaped amphorae with long narrow necks, globular pyxides on very high feet, little one-handled jugs, and askoi.

In the Caltagirone necropolis cylindrical pyxides, four-handled hydriai with hemispherical lids, and 'tea-pots' with

Plate 61

Fig. 31

strainer spouts are also found. While some of these forms can still be attributed to the tradition of the preceding Thapsos culture, others like the tea⁄pot, the four⁄handled hydria, etc., show clear Mycenaean influence. Of probable Mycenaean inspiration are the gold finger⁄rings with settings decorated

Plates 56, 58

with an interlaced scroll motif or with an apotropaic eye, or with a fish, specimens of which came from Pantalica, Caltagi⁄rone and Dessueri. The same Mycenaean stamp is found in the bronzes.

Fig. 33, a
Fig. 32, d
Fig. 33, b–d

The earliest tombs at Pantalica produce round mirrors, small knives with handle and blade cast in one piece, and swords of types which still seem to belong to a Mycenaean III B tradition (about 1300–1230 B.C.) rather than to the sub⁄Mycenaean period (Mycenaean III C, about 1230–1100 B.C.).

The large number of bronze objects which one finds in every tomb of this period clearly shows that metal was no longer a rarity, as it still was in the Thapsos period when it was practi⁄cally limited to the making of weapons and a few ornamental objects; now it is widely used for everyday purposes. In almost

Fig. 32, c

every tomb we find little knives with flame⁄shaped blades, and razors of a very particular type, with narrow blade and slightly

Fig. 32, e, g

concave sides, so far known almost only from Sicily.

But from the chronological standpoint the most significant object and the one which is most helpful to the archaeologist for dating the grave⁄goods is the big safety⁄pin, or fibula, which was used to fasten the cloak. In this earliest phase these fibulae

Fig. 32, h
Fig. 32, a, b

were still sometimes shaped like a violin bow, but more usually they are of the simple arc type, often with little knobs at their ends. At Caltagirone one side of the arc is often straight.

The imported Mycenaean objects which had been so fre⁄quently found in the preceding period are altogether absent in the Sicilian necropoleis of this period. The commercial exchanges between the Aegean and Sicily must have slowed down considerably, even if they had not altogether stopped.

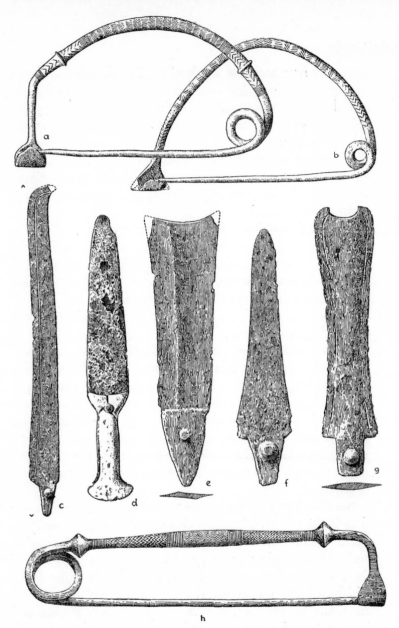

Fig. 32   Characteristic bronzes of the Pantalica North-Caltagirone period, from the Pantalica necropoleis. Length of (c) 6¼", others to scale. Syracuse Museum.

Fig. 33 (a) bronze mirror from the Pantalica North necropolis, tomb 37; (b, c) bronze daggers from Dessueri; (d) bronze dagger from Pantalica South, tomb 124. Length of (d) 7½", others to scale.

Fig. 34

Fig. 41, f

But as we have seen, the whole of the Pantalica period shows signs of very strong Mycenaean influence, and we shall see in due course how this manifests itself not only in the pottery and objects of domestic use, but also in the architecture of the princely palaces.

In contrast to this, nothing in the Pantalica civilization, at least in the necropoleis which we have chosen to investigate, seems to remind us of the Apennine or sub-Apennine cultures of the Italian mainland.

Phase II (about 1000–850 B.C.) is represented at Pantalica only by the contents of a few tombs. On the other hand, all the tombs in the large Cassibile necropolis belong to it, as well as many of those at Dessueri, the Mulino della Badia necropolis near Grammichele in the Caltagirone district, that of Calcarella at Calascibetta near Enna, etc. This is the phase which we can call the 'Cassibile phase'.

The red pottery disappears, and in its place there is a painted ware with very characteristic plume motifs, closely resembling that which we have already described from the Ausonian II phase in Lipari. Some of the forms are evidently derived from types of the preceding phase, while others, as for instance the little bucket-shaped pots, are entirely new. Much the commonest form at Cassibile is the plate on a very tall stand, which might perhaps have been a lamp set to light the nether world of the dead.

But the change in the bronze types is even more noticeable than in the pottery. The fibula characteristic of this phase is the stilted one, sometimes bent into a loop, generally very massive, and with a straight pin: a type which we have already seen in the Ausonian huts on the Lipari acropolis. It is the fibula which in Sicily we can call the 'Cassibile fibula'. The simple arc fibula is still used, but its arc is generally thicker and heavier. Together with the fibulae, we find a little knife with a curved blade and looped handle, also typical of this period.

The Pantalica razor disappears, and is replaced by new types: one with a thin roundish or rectangular blade, typical of the proto-Villanovan necropoleis of the Italian peninsula, and also found at Milazzo; the other, a leaf-shaped type, known from

Fig. 41, 1

Fig. 35 (7)

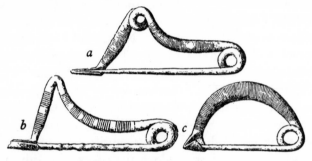

Fig. 34 Characteristic fibulae of the Cassibile period from the Dessueri necropolis. Length of (a) 3¾″, others to scale.

the Iberian peninsula. The shaft-hole axe is now found for the first time.

Fig. 41, e

The bronzes of the Cassibile period are of the greatest interest for the correlations they enable us to make between Sicily and the other Mediterranean regions, some of them linking Sicily to the East. The typical stilted fibula is, in fact, known from Megiddo (Palestine) in the tenth century B.C. and from Cyprus. The less common one, which has its pin detached from the arc, found in some hoards of this period, recurs in Crete.

But many more comparisons draw us towards the West: it is curious how several of the Sicilian bronzes of this age recur in Spain or on the Atlantic coasts of France and England. A hoard at Huelva in Andalusia provides us with fibulae which, though somewhat more elaborate, substantially reproduce the stilted type of Cassibile. In another hoard at Huerta de Arriba near Burgos there are leaf-shaped razors comparable to many in the British Isles and identical with a specimen from Cassibile, and fibulae with pin detached from the arc. From the Syracuse neighbourhood comes a palstave of a type almost unique in Sicily but widely diffused in the Iberian peninsula as well as in the hoard of Huerta de Arriba itself. Stilted or looped fibulae were in the hoards from Nôtre Dame d'Ors (Poitiers) and Venât (Angoulême); shaft-hole axes of the Sicilian type have been recovered as far afield as Nantes and England. Other examples could easily be added. These typological analogies are certainly not accidental; on the contrary, they are archaeo-logical reflections of a historical fact of wide significance: Phoenician navigation and commerce in the west Mediter-ranean and beyond the Straits of Gibraltar.

We are in the tenth and ninth centuries B.C., in the period of Phoenician colonization along the coasts of North Africa and Spain. Utica and Cadiz have already been founded; the Phoenician ships have taken the place of the Mycenaean ones in the seas around Sicily.

Phase III (about 850–730 B.C.). This is represented, above all, by the necropoleis of Filiporto, Cavetta; and south, at Pantalica, by a group of tombs at Centuripe, by some of the earliest tombs at Monte Finocchito, by the Cozzo San Giuseppe necropolis at Realmese near Calascibetta, etc.

The type of tomb tends to change, and in contrast to the hitherto exclusive little oven-shaped chamber, the rectangular chamber with a flat roof, always of about the same size, becomes more and more common.

Fig. 36

The pottery alters markedly. Forms evidently influenced by Greek geometric types, like the trilobe-mouthed 'oinochoai',
sometimes with a high neck, or the big carinated bowls are
Fig. 36, a, e
now found. The askos grows increasingly common, while the
Fig. 36, d
schnabelkanne is sometimes present. The plumed decoration lingers on, but very often associated with a design of parallel grooves, made on the wheel. There is also a class of grey ware,
Fig. 36, b, d
with a very restrained decoration made with a wooden spatula.

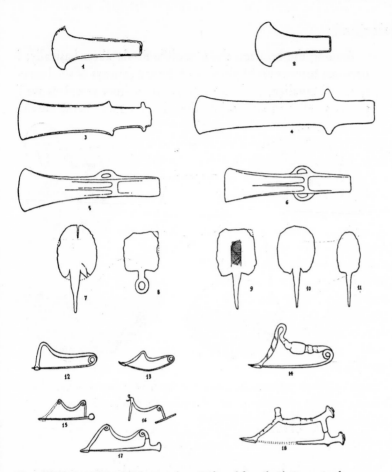

Fig. 35 Characteristic bronzes from Sicily and from the Iberian peninsula:

(1) *from Vizzini. Syracuse Museum* (2) *from Portugal*

(3) *from the Modica hoard* (4) *from Coruna del Conde*

(5) *axe from Syracuse. Palermo Museum* (6) *axe from the hoard of Huerto de Arriba*

(7) *razor from Cassibile* (8) *razor from Mulino della Badia*

(9–11) *razors from the Huerta de Arriba hoard* (12, 13) *fibulae from Cassibile*

(14) *fibula from the Huelva hoard*

(15, 16) *fibulae from the Noto and Priolo hills. Syracuse Museum*

(17) *fibula. Palermo Museum* (18) *fibula from Spain*

Among the bronzes, the Cassibile fibula alters basically; it becomes thinner and lighter, and the arc (always of the looped type at Pantalica, and at Realmese sometimes stilted as well) grows smaller in size, while the pin gets longer and curved.

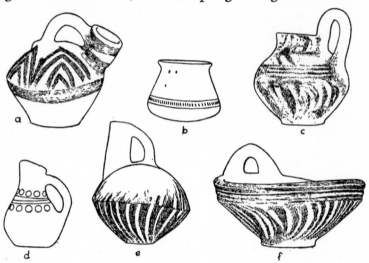

Fig. 36 *Characteristic pottery from the Pantalica South necropolis:*
(a) *with painted geometric decoration (Height 6", others to scale);*
(b, d) *with incised decoration;*
(c, e, f) *with painted 'plumed' decoration.*
Syracuse Museum.

Fig. 37

Little rings, buttons, disc- or cylinder-spirals, etc., become very common.

Phase IV (about 730–650 B.C.). The fourth period can be called the Finocchito period, because most tombs in this necropolis belong to it, as well as those of Giummarito, Tremenzano, Noto Vecchio, etc. It is the period to which one should also refer the many rock-cut tombs around Lentini (Cava Ruccia, Cava Sant' Eligio) and Militello (Ossini). But the richest and most significant discovery of this period is perhaps that of the two tombs in Via Polara at Modica.

By now, the indigenous civilization is quickly being altered through contact with the superior civilization of the Greeks, who have already founded, or are founding, their colonies on the coasts of Sicily.

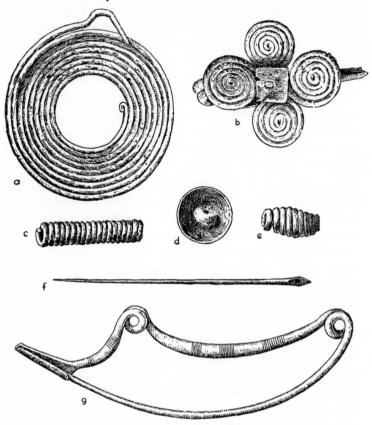

Fig. 37   Characteristic bronzes from Pantalica South necropolis:

(a) *disc-shaped spiral*   (b) *cruciform fibula of four spirals*
(c) *cylindrical spiral*   (d) *hemispherical button*
(e) *biconical spiral*   (f) *needle with eye. Length $3\frac{7}{8}''$, others to scale*
                 (g) *looped fibula with curved pin.*

Syracuse Museum.

The products of Greek industry and craftsmanship are spreading and being widely imitated, and they are stimulating many local industries as well. A beautiful painted ware now begins to appear, inspired by late geometric Greek prototypes, both in its forms and in its decorative motifs. Figures are very rare, being limited to a few stylized birds. Found with this pottery there is an incised ware, often with geometric motifs. Its charac-teristic form is the big straight-sided bowl with three or four ring handles, evidently an imitation of a bronze prototype.

Plate 62

Plate 63

The commonest fibula at this time is of Greek type and has a small lozenge-shaped arc and a long catch-plate; associated with it is the serpentine fibula with its arc bordered with little rods. Ornamental rings of various sizes are very common, and so are oval or biconical bronze beads, necklaces, or bracelets made of single or double mesh chain, and pendants of various shapes. It is only now that iron begins to be used for making knives, arrow-heads and, above all, for fibulae: no doubt it was a contribution from Greek civilization.

Fig. 38

Greek objects are found in the tombs at Finocchito and Modica: little proto-Corinthian pots, ivory or bone fibulae, absolutely identical in type to those of the earliest tombs or the first votive deposits of Greek Syracuse. These show the contem-poraneity between the Finocchito culture and the first phases of development in the earliest Greek colonies in Sicily.

In contact with the superior Greek civilization, the Siculan peoples quickly lost their own individuality; the Finocchito culture soon changed into that of Licodia Eubea, widely permeated now by Greek influences, though retaining a number of its own characteristics, both in its tombs, of the subterranean-chamber type, and in the types of its pottery, household goods, bronzes, etc. We can follow the evolution of this culture from the middle of the seventh until the end of the fifth century B.C., by which time the cultural levelling in Sicily can be regarded as complete, even if the standard of life

Fig. 38 Ornamental bronze chains from the Finocchito necropolis (Noto).
Depth of top ornament just under 6″, others to scale.
Syracuse Museum.

161

in the bigger Greek centres on the coasts differs from that of the Siculo-Greek towns of the interior.

But this late evolution in indigenous culture at the time when Greek civilization was flourishing in Sicily lies outside the scope of our researches.

4. THE MAIN ARCHAEOLOGICAL CENTRES IN SOUTH-EASTERN SICILY

The discoveries relating to this long period of Sicilian proto-history are very numerous, and it would be impossible to make a complete and detailed examination of them.

We will limit ourselves, therefore, to making a rapid survey of the main centres, beginning in the south-eastern corner, which is the best explored part of the island.

The largest and most well-known habitation site of this period is undoubtedly Pantalica, and thus it has more claim than any other to give its name to the East Sicilian civilization of this time. Pantalica lies on a mountain spur, completely isolated on all sides by the very deep valleys of the Anapo and the Calcinara, one of its smaller tributaries; it is joined to the plateau behind only by the narrow saddle of Filiporto which, later, in Greek times, was barred by a strong fortification. The Pantalica plateau towers above the surrounding valleys with very high rocky cliffs, inaccessible except at a few points. So Pantalica is a real natural fortress, of far greater extent than those of the Milazzese promontory in Panarea, of Portella in Salina, or the Lipari acropolis. It has an area of twenty acres and a perimeter of three miles. Its defensive value was therefore conditioned by its having a sufficiently large garrison to man all its vulnerable points, and it must, in fact, have had a large population.

We know nothing of the houses except an *Anaktoron*, or

prince's palace, built of large polygonal blocks in a megalithic style, reminding one, on a small scale, of the palaces of the Mycenaean world. It shows that power must have been firmly concentrated in the hands of one king or *anax*.

Plate 65
Fig. 39

Sandstone moulds for casting axes and other bronze objects

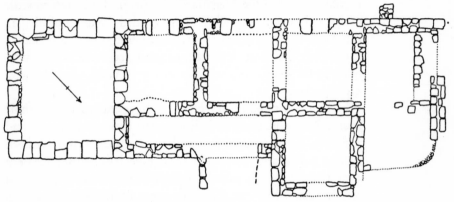

Fig. 39   Plan of the Anaktoron of Pantalica. Length, 116 ft.

were discovered in one of its rooms, and make us wonder whether the metal-working carried on here may not have been one of the prerogatives of the sovereign power at this time.

A mass of rock-cut tombs can be seen in the cliffs surrounding the whole site, numbering more than five thousand, and making these cliffs look like enormous honeycombs. They are grouped together in five large necropoleis, two of which, those of Pantalica North and North-west, belong in the main to the earliest phase of the site, i.e. to the thirteenth–eleventh centuries B.C. The other three, i.e. those of Filiporto, of Pantalica South, and of Cavetta, on the other hand, belong chiefly to the third phase (about 850–730 B.C.). Only a few of the tombs so far excavated can be referred to the second period (about 1000–850 B.C.), but that may be largely accidental. The tombs belonging to the latest phase, that of the Greek colonization (*post* 730 B.C.), are still few in number. Possibly the growing

Plate 64

importance of Syracuse, and its expansion into the hinterland, led to the depopulation of Pantalica.

It has recently been suggested by François Villard that Pantalica (whose present name is probably of Byzantine origin) can be identified with the legendary Hybla, whose king, Hyblon, allowed the Megarian colonists under Lamis to settle in that strip of territory where they founded the town of Megara Hyblaea. The hypothesis is very convincing, because Pantalica is not only the most important of pre-Greek centres in Sicily, but also the nearest of them to the strip of coast where Megara Hyblaea lay.

Hyblon's kingdom will certainly have included the whole Monte Lauro plateau, and all the coast between Augusta and Syracuse, but the greater part of the population must have been centred at Pantalica itself. The coast, especially, must have been almost uninhabited, with the exception of the small settlement on Ortygia, which we shall talk about later. The economy of these peoples will have been based on the hills of the hinter-land, as is explicitly confirmed by the written sources (Strabo, *VI, 2, 4*).

Though somewhat scattered, there must have been, on the higher country outside the town, some small inhabited nuclei, attested today by groups of tombs at Rivettazzo (Pantalica, stage I), and Bosco Rotondo (Pantalica, stage III).

The most outstanding of these must have been on the very place which was later chosen for the Syracusan colony of Akrai. Its existence there is shown by the small necropolis of Pinita of some fifty tombs whose exact date is uncertain, since they have all lost their grave-goods; typologically, however, they seem to be early.

We know from Thucydides that when they were founding Syracuse, the Corinthians under Archias drove out the Sikels from Ortygia, the island which they occupied, and which has since then always been the nucleus of the town. Orsi's excavations near the Athenaion, the largest temple in the town, revealed remains of two oval huts belonging to the Siculan site in Ortygia, while some chamber-tombs had previously been found near the Fountain of Arethusa.

The material from the huts belonged to the period imme- diately before the founding of Syracuse by the Greeks, i.e. to our third phase (850–730 B.C.).

Another of the main pre-Greek centres of eastern Sicily is at Cassibile. At the point where the river of the same name flows out of a narrow gorge into the strip of coastal plain, the very steep mountain slopes flanking it are riddled with about two thousand tombs of the usual type; some of these are in clusters, others more scattered. No signs of houses have so far been found, so that the location of the settlement is doubtful. The material recovered from these tombs all belongs to one period: the second of our classification, and the one in fact which is called after Cassibile (about 1000–850 B.C.). No traces of either the earlier or later periods have been found. Cassibile, in spite of its great size, seems therefore to have had a relatively short life.

Plate 66

The third of the big protohistoric centres in the Syracuse district is at Monte Finocchito. Here, just as at Pantalica, the dwellings occupied the top of an isolated hill on the southern edge of the Akrai plateau towards the valley of the Tellaro; it was about five miles, as the crow flies, south-east of Castelluccio.

The position in this case was even stronger than at Castel- luccio, because the hill was surrounded by steeper valleys and bounded by less accessible cliffs. The narrow saddle joining this hill to the plateau was barred by a strong fortification, perhaps the earliest work of its kind known in Sicily; it consisted of a large dry-stone wall forming two curved bastions. In the sur- rounding cliffs, and also at some distance from the habitation site, there were numerous groups of tombs (several hundred of them in all), some of which were still of the roundish vaulted type. But most were small, rectangular rooms with a flat roof and without forecourt or niches. Some of them had side benches on which were placed the heads of the skeletons, generally not more than two or three, that lay full length, or with their legs slightly bent.

Some of the tombs from their looped arc fibulae and pottery types still belonged evidently to the Pantalica South period, but most of the grave-goods with their long catch-plate fibulae and with their wealth of rings, chains, biconical bronze beads and iron objects belong rather to the period called after Monte Finocchito (750–650 B.C.). Fibulae were also found here with iron frames and amber or bone sheaths, identical with those from the earliest Greek tombs at Syracuse and Megara Hyblaea, and large ivory plaques such as those from the votive deposit of the Athenaion at Syracuse.

Other small tomb groups of the same age, e.g. those at Cozzo delle Giummare and at Murmuro a few miles from Monte Finocchito, show that small villages had existed around the main settlement. A little to the west of Castelluccio, but still on the edge of the Akrai plateau, is another little site of the same period known as Tremenzano. The ancient town of Neaiton (Noto Vecchio, about six miles from the modern town of Noto) was also already in existence in the Finocchito period. This town, which lasted until the earthquake of 1693, occupied an isolated rocky hill-top between two deep valleys, and in the steep cliffs around it, specially on the south, were large numbers of chamber-tombs which produced grave-goods coeval with those from Monte Finocchito.

Probably Motyke (the present Modica) and Hybla Heraia (Ragusa) also existed at this time. At Modica, in fact, in Via Polara, two tombs were discovered which yielded a conspi-cuous number of geometric painted pots in the Finocchito style. These are amongst the best of the indigenous products of this period. There were also numerous long catch-plated

Fig. 38

Plate 63

fibulae, small chains, etc. With these there was a small proto-
Corinthian cup, datable to the end of the eighth century B.C.,
and this provides a valuable element in the dating of the group.

Caltagirone was another of the large pre-Greek centres. In
the whole of the area north of the modern town, in the districts
known as 'La Montagna' and 'La Rocca', there are numbers
of tombs of this period. Orsi thought there were more than
1,500.

As a matter of fact, it is only in a few places that they are
concentrated in huge necropoleis, such as those at Pantalica
and Cassibile. As a rule, large steep rock-faces in which
similar tombs could have been cut were not to be found. Here
one is dealing, rather, with countless little groups of rock-cut
tombs, spread over an area of about three miles by one and a
half, made wherever there was a small outcrop of soft limestone.

Some of these tombs are earlier: a few of them date back to
the Early Bronze Age, but most of them belong to the same
age as the north and north-west necropoleis at Pantalica, and
produce the same monochrome glossy red pottery, even if the
forms are sometimes noticeably different. The most character-   *Fig. 31*
istic of these are the four-handled hydria, often with a hemispherical lid, the 'tea-pot' and the cylindrical pyxis: at least
the first two of these forms are clearly of Mycenaean derivation.

Among the bronze objects are simple arc fibulae, daggers,
a big sword, etc. There are also two gold rings whose settings
are decorated either with a plaited motif evidently of Mycenaean   Plate 58
influence, or with an apotropaic eye.   Plate 56

Some of the Caltagirone tombs are of great interest from an
architectural point of view, because of their very regular tholos
form, which distinguishes them from all other Sicilian tombs.
In some respects it links them, even if on a small scale, to the
Mycenaean prototypes.

A few of the tombs belong to a later date, i.e. to that of the
south necropolis at Pantalica (about 850–730 B.C.).

It is difficult to establish the exact position of the dwelling site corresponding to this great necropolis, because no signs of it have so far been found.

The country round Calascibetta, at a short distance from Enna, and right in the middle of Sicily, was also intensely inhabited in protohistoric times. Recently, systematic exploration here has led to the discovery of various necropoleis, ranging in time between the tenth and the sixth centuries B.C. The earliest of these is Calcarella, consisting of about 130 tombs, rock-cut, and almost all circular, though a few of them are quadrangular and belong mostly to the Cassibile period. They have produced some stilted fibulae.

Another, larger, necropolis, not far from the last-named one, is at Cozzo San Giuseppe near Realmese. Here the tombs, numbering over three hundred, were circular and sometimes quadrangular, and the material from them belongs to a later date. The looped fibula, a type characteristic of Pantalica South, is predominant here, while the long catch-plate fibula is still absent. But the pottery is related in style to the West Sicilian horizon of Sant' Angelo Muxaro, rather than to the eastern one of Pantalica-Finocchito.

Plate 69

The last of the large necropoleis of this period, still linked typologically with eastern Sicily, is that of Dessueri, situated at a point in which the river of the same name flows out into the plain of Gela, where its course has recently been dammed in order to make an artificial lake. Its tombs, more than two thousand of them, are thickly clustered on the rocky sides of Monte Dessueri and Monte Canalotto and are particularly numerous at the points locally known as La Palombara (the dove-cote) and Fastuccheria.

The grave-goods from Dessueri all belong to the archaic phases, i.e. to the phases of Pantalica North and Cassibile. Both red and plumed ware are common there, as well as their corresponding bronzes. There are no traces of later objects.

When life came to an end at Dessueri it probably began at Butera, a town in a very strong position dominating the Gela plain from the north-west. The earliest tombs at the large necropolis of Piano della Fiera, little rooms dug out of the very friable rock, belong to the pre-Greek period, i.e. to that of Pantalica South, with which they share the same characteristic fibulae. But the pottery is very different from that of eastern Sicily, and belongs rather to types characteristic of the west of the island.

A second stratum of tombs, overlying the earlier ones, definitely belongs to the beginning of Greek colonization: to a period, that is, following the foundation of near-by Gela. These tombs sometimes contained inhumations, and sometimes cremations, with the ashes collected in *pithoi* with plumed decorations, and they produced the first proto-Corinthian vases.

5. NORTHERN INFLUENCES ON EASTERN SICILY: FROM LEONTINOI TO MULINO DELLA BADIA

This assemblage of discoveries ranging from Pantalica to Dessueri, and including the whole of south-eastern Sicily, shows a fairly homogeneous cultural *facies*. Both the types of pottery and the bronzes are constantly repeated age after age, all over this vast territory. The unmistakable Mycenaean influences which distinguish the first stage are later replaced by Phoenician ones. In the third stage imitations of late geometric Greek types prevail, whereas the funeral rites, just like many other elements, continue to be the ones which had been traditional in Sicily since the Early and Middle Bronze Ages.

But not one of these elements is reminiscent of those Apennine or sub-Apennine cultures of the Italian mainland, which the sources would lead us to expect were brought by the Sikels. South-eastern Sicily, during the Late Bronze Age and the

Early Iron Age, looked towards the Mediterranean and Greece rather than to Italy. We shall find parallels to the Pantalica grave-goods more easily in the earliest tombs of the Kerameikos cemetery at Athens than in the late Apennine villages or in the proto-Villanovan urnfields of the Italian mainland. And yet there can be no doubt that the people living in south-eastern Sicily at the time when the Greeks were founding their first colonies, and who, coming in contact with them, quickly absorbed their customs and lore, were those people whom the Greeks knew as Sikels. We must conclude that if the Sikels really are the Italic people mentioned by the sources, they must, after having conquered Sicily, have themselves been culturally absorbed by the superior civilization of their subject peoples, thereby losing both their cultural and ethnic individuality.

Their influence on south-eastern Sicily would seem to have been more negative than positive. It seems, in fact, to have shown itself not in the contribution of new techniques, usages, styles, or ideas, so much as in the fact that it forced the indigenous peoples, by the threat of raids and the need for self-defence, to accept very hard conditions of life.

In contrast to the Ausonians of Lipari and Milazzo, who preserved intact for a long time the cultural heritage which they had brought with them, the Sikels soon seem to have abandoned their culture and to have accepted that of the vanquished peoples.

Although the groups of sites and necropoleis which we have so far been discussing is perhaps the richest in Sicily, it is nevertheless only a part of the island's cultural panorama. In fact, Sicily seems at this time to have been a very complex cultural world with marked regional differences and a variety of aspects. Nor is this complex lacking in features which are evidently in discord with those we have so far noted and which can more closely be related to the cultures of the Italian mainland and the Aeolian Islands.

Recently, in the area of Greek Naxos, a cylinder handle has been found which is of Apennine type and characteristic of Ausonian I in Lipari. Another similar one comes from Tyndaris. But among less typical material from the Paternò acropolis was a horned handle shaped like an animal's head, similar to those of Ausonian II. Thus the north-eastern point of Sicily seems, to judge from the little so far known, to have been more open to cultural influences coming from the Italian mainland and the Aeolian Islands, although at the Paternò acropolis which was certainly an inhabited centre of no small importance (perhaps Hybla Galeatis) characteristic south-eastern Sicilian types were also found: i.e. the glossy red pottery of the Pantalica North style, plumed Cassibile ware, etc.

Another important centre must have existed in the neigh-bourhood of Mendolito near Adrano, on the lower Etna slopes towards the Simeto river: an anonymous town, still archaeo-logically unexplored, but from which come the most important inscriptions in the Siculan language so far known, as well as the biggest hoard of bronzes yet found in Sicily. Some fibulae and other bronzes from this site show that it was already in existence at least at the time of Pantalica South (850–730 B.C.).

A site of remarkable importance existed at what was later to be the Greek Leontinoi. It is possible that this was Xuthia, the town founded by Xouthos, one of the Aeolids descended from Liparos. A little while ago only the tombs were known from this site, all of them of the rock-cut type made in the steep sides of the narrow parallel valleys of Sant' Eligio and Cava Ruccia that flank the town on two sides. From these tombs came an important collection of painted pottery: besides the usual geometric patterns, some of these sherds had bird figures as well. The long catch-plate fibulae show that they definitely belong to the very early stages of Greek colonization, i.e. to the Finocchito period to which the pottery must also be stylistically related.

Plate 62

171

It seems, therefore, that these tombs must either just antedate the arrival of the Greeks, or that they may belong to a group of Sikels living side by side with the first Greek colonists, and preserving to a certain extent their own cultural and ethnic individuality. Recent excavations on the Meta Piccola hill, one of the hills later to come within the precincts of Greek Leon- tinoi, have brought to light a group of huts which certainly date back to a somewhat earlier time, i.e. to the period preced- ing the Greek colonization. These huts are, in fact, almost contemporary with those of the Athenaion of Syracuse, though they are of a rather different type, being rectangular and not round. They were evidently largely built of wood, and around them in the ground were the post-holes of the framework and of the door-jambs, and sometimes of a small porch. The floors

Plates 67, 68

Fig. 40

were somewhat lower than the surrounding ground. Inside each hut there was always a hearth.

These huts are very like those found on the Palatine at Rome, and those of which slight traces remain on the Lipari acropolis: in fact, they are of the Italic type.

The anonymous town in the Ossini–San Lio neighbour- hood, about half-way between Francofonte and Militello, showed a cultural panorama not very different from that of Lentini. Protected all round by deep valleys, it must have looked like a small version of Pantalica. Its origin seems to have been very ancient, since objects of the Copper Age and Early Bronze Age were found there; but it had a remarkable development in the Finocchito period, for it produced painted pottery analogous to that from Lentini as well as proto- Corinthian ware of the late eighth and the first half of the seventh centuries B.C.

A most unusual position in Sicilian protohistory is held by the vast necropolis of Mulino della Badia near Grammichele in the Caltagirone district. Here we find funeral rites com- pletely different from any which have so far been found in the island. It is, in fact, a necropolis of inhumation tombs with the bodies laid on their backs in simple graves dug in the ground, usually with a few stones set round the head for protection, or occasionally with stones all round the body. Besides this type of grave, there were also two burials with skeletons in big

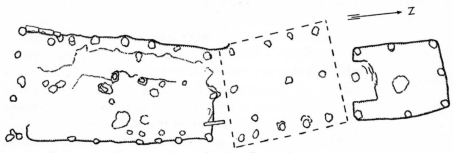

Fig. 40 Plan of three rectangular huts from the village on the Meta Piccola hill at Lentini. 70 ft. long.

amphorae, of the same type as the Middle Bronze Age ones at Milazzo and those of Ausonian II at Lipari.

Most of the tombs in this necropolis had been plundered by peasants, but a few were systematically excavated by Orsi.

In contrast to the small amount of pottery, almost all with plumed decoration, the bronzes from here are very numerous; the fibulae include the following types: simple arc, arc with one straight side, harp-shaped (*j*), stilted (*a*) and looped, but all of them have a straight pin. There are also large quantities of little loop-handled knives (*f*) and rectangular bladed razors (*l*), and associated with these are some curious little hollow cylinders (*g, i*) and ribbon-shaped perforated blades (*b*), never seen elsewhere and of unknown use and significance. No tomb seems to be later than the Cassibile period.

As a matter of fact, the Mulino della Badia necropolis, even if the type of its graves makes it a novelty in the prehistoric panorama of Sicily, is typically Sicilian in most of its bronze

Fig. 41

types and its plumed pottery. It is only linked to the Italian mainland by a few bronze types such as razors (*l*), belt-clasps (*k*) and little daggers of 'Peschiera' type (*c*).

6. THE LATE BRONZE AND THE IRON AGE IN CENTRAL AND WESTERN SICILY

At the time when the Greeks founded their first colonies in the last third of the eighth century B.C., Sicily was divided ethnically into two large regions: the eastern, inhabited by the Sikels, and the western by the Sikans. Still farther to the west were the Elymians in the territory corresponding to the present province of Trapani and part of that of Palermo.

At that time it might have seemed that the boundary between the Sikels and the Sikans was on the South Himera river (now called the Salso), but it is known that the Sikans had previously spread over a much larger territory, from which they had gradu- ally been driven farther and farther westwards by the Sikels. The fact is that, while all the ancient sources are in agreement over the origins of the Sikels, describing them as a people who had migrated from the Italian mainland, our information about the Sikans and the Elymians is much less clear.

The traditions concerning the origins of the Sikans are very much at variance. Some of the ancient writers (Timaeus and Diodorus) claim that they were autochthonous, and as such they regarded themselves. Others, as for instance Thucydides and Philistus the Syracusan, basing their deductions on imaginary relationships between Sicilian and Iberian place- names, considered them to have been Iberians who had migrated into Sicily through Italy. According to yet another tradition, they had once lived in Latium and were related to the Sikels who were shortly after to follow them into Sicily.

It was said (Diodorus, *V, 6*) that the Sikans had originally lived in eastern Sicily as well, but that, frightened by the terrible

and insistent eruptions of Etna, they had later moved westwards, and the territory they relinquished was occupied by the
Sikels. Diodorus tells us that they used to live in villages, and

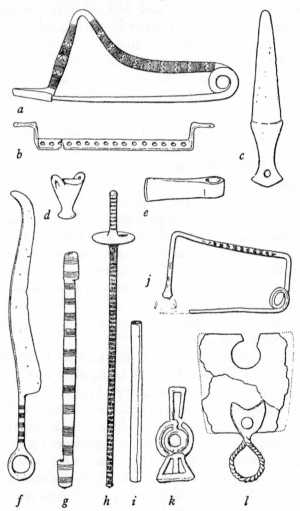

*Fig. 41   Characteristic bronzes from the Mulino della Badia necropolis (Grammichele).
Length of (a) 4⅞″, others to scale.*

built their strongholds on steep mountains to defend themselves from marauding raiders. We know practically nothing about their towns: Kamikos, Inykon, Hykkara, Omphakê, Indara, Krastos, Ouessa, Miskera and Makara; only the sites of Kamikos and Makara are possibly identifiable today.

As far as the Elymians are concerned, there are two traditions. One of them, handed down to us by Dionysius of Halicarnassus from the earlier sources of Hellanicus of Mytilene, would have it that they came from Italy a few years before the Sikels; the other, which was followed by Thucydides (*VI, 2*), regarded them as a locally formed group, descended from a cross between some Trojans who had fled from the Achaeans after the fall of Troy, and the local Sikans, with the possible addition of some Phocians who had also fled from Troy. The value of these legends, as well as of those relating to the Sikans, is very dubious. From the archaeological point of view, western Sicily differs very markedly from the east. This divergence becomes both stronger and clearer as time goes on, till it reaches a climax around the time of the first Greek colonies and shortly after.

The evolution of the western Sicilian cultures is so far less clear than that of the eastern ones, due both to the lesser number of discoveries and to the rather haphazard methods by which some of them were achieved.

We have already mentioned the Caldare tombs in the Agrigento district, which could be regarded as transitional between the Middle and Late Bronze Ages.

In the Syracuse Museum there is a small group of bronzes from some oven-shaped tombs discovered about 1880 by L. Mauceri near Valledolmo in the province of Caltanissetta. It includes two fibulae still very close to the most archaic violin-bow type, a knife with a bone handle analogous to those from the earliest tombs of Pantalica North, and two swords similar to the ones from Caldare.

Another important centre of this period in the Agrigento

district is Cannatello, a vast dwelling site tentatively explored by Mosso, who recognized remains of huts and of coarsely paved roads there. The pottery from this site has not so far enabled us to establish very precise correlations with other *facies* known in Sicilian protohistory, but fortunately the same site has produced a group of very important bronzes, including two daggers like the Caldare ones, two shaft-hole axes, four spear-heads, etc.

Perhaps at some time rather later than that to which we should refer the Caldare and Cannatello finds, the Sant' Angelo Muxaro culture was developing in western Sicily. This we can regard as the counterpart of the East Sicilian cultures of Cassibile, Pantalica South and Monte Finocchito.

The best-known centre of this culture is at Sant' Angelo Muxaro itself, which one would like to recognize as the ancient Kamikos, to which the legends of King Kokalos relate. It was to his court that Daedalus fled from Crete to escape from the wrath of Minos. King Kokalos, who was at that time reigning over the city of Inykon, welcomed the refugee artist and made him build the impregnable stronghold of Kamikos which had such a narrow and well-defended entrance that a mere three or four guards could man it. Here Kokalos built his palace and collected his treasures, but Minos, still pursuing Daedalus, carried the war even as far as Sicily. Landing with a powerful fleet at Makara, later called Minoa, he sent messengers to Kokalos, asking him to punish Daedalus. Kokalos, much concerned, decided to resort to deception, and having invited Minos to his palace, he had him suffocated in the bath; he then sent his body back to the Cretans, pretending that his death was accidental. The Cretans erected a magnificent monument to him, and on it they built a temple to Aphrodite, which was much venerated for a long time by the Sikans until it was destroyed by Theron the tyrant of Akragas. But after the death of Minos the Cretans were left without a ruler, and discord broke out. The Sikans, taking advantage of the situation, set fire to the Cretans' ships and so made it impossible for them to return home. They thereupon decided to remain in the island. Some of them stayed on in Makara itself, which they called Minoa; others pushed farther inland and, taking possession of a high place, founded a town called Engyon.

Orsi's excavations at Sant' Angelo Muxaro brought to light an outstanding series of chamber-tombs ranging in date over several centuries. The earliest of them (tombs VII to XIX), set at the foot of the hill, were smaller than the others, and pro-duced pottery and bronzes of still very archaic types. The razors and a bronze dagger are still typologically similar to the ones from Pantalica North, but the pottery seems to be closer to that from Cassibile. It might be thought, therefore, that this western zone lagged behind the eastern one, and that in the west the Pantalica type of razor continued to be used for longer.

Some other tombs, rather higher up the very steep Muxaro hill-side, are different from all other Sicilian tombs of this type. Not only do they almost always have two rooms, but they also attain very grandiose dimensions; the largest of them, which in Byzantine times was turned into a chapel dedicated to the cult of Sant' Angelo, measured twenty-six feet in diameter by nearly ten feet in height. These are, in fact, real tholoi, comparable with the Mycenaean ones, though, as is always the case in Sicily, they are dug out of the soft, chalky limestone, and not built above ground as in Greece.

Some of these tombs contained a real funeral bed, standing alone; on it the body was originally laid, while many other bodies were placed on the ground around, together with an enormous quantity of pottery. The Sant' Angelo tomb had a kind of bench all round the inside. The grave-goods from these fine tombs show that they were in use over several centuries, perhaps from the eighth to the middle of the fifth century B.C.

These later tombs produced very characteristic pottery which is altogether different from that from eastern Sicily; a first group consists of little pots finely incised with geometric motifs, and with small concentric circles or other impressed designs. The smaller pots of this kind are almost always brown or blackish, while the bigger ones, among which are some large high-footed cups, are generally red. Belonging apparently to a somewhat later date is a monochrome red ware whose most characteristic form is an ovoid, wide-mouthed jar. And finally there is a painted ware that is evidently an imitation of Corinthian and Rhodian prototypes of the orientalizing period, and which therefore cannot be dated before the end of the seventh century B.C. and after. It is with this later material of the sixth century B.C. that we should connect the splendid gold rings with animal figures incised in their settings. They seem to descend from remote Mycenaean traditions rather than to have been inspired by Greek prototypes.

The contemporary village of Polizello near Mussomeli is closely related to Sant' Angelo Muxaro. In the eighth and possibly also in the first half of the seventh century B.C., the Sant' Angelo Muxaro and Polizello cultural *facies* actually extended farther to the east of the boundary dividing the Sikels from the Sikans in the fully historical period. At Butera, on the edge of the Gela plain, and to the east of the Himera river, the Piano della Fiera necropolis, about which we have already spoken, produced the Sant' Angelo Muxaro style incised pottery associated in the tombs with little Greek pots of proto-Corinthian style or of a style transitional between the proto-Corinthian and the Corinthian decorated with animals. This necropolis must therefore have continued in use at least all through the seventh century B.C.

Near Calascibetta, in the Cozzo San Giuseppe necropolis at Realmese, the Sant' Angelo Muxaro incised pottery was characteristic of the tombs with fibulae of eighth-century B.C.,

Plate 73

Plates 70, 71

Plate 72

Fig. 42 Handles with schematized faces from Segesta. Half actual size.

pre-Greek type, while the rather later ones showing clear Greek influence contained pottery of East Sicilian type ranging chrono-logically from the Monte Finocchito culture to that of Licodia Eubea. The near-by necropolis of Valle Coniglio, both in the type of its square chamber-tombs and in the style of its pottery, comes fully within the range of the Licodia Eubea culture.

During the seventh century B.C., therefore, this central Sicilian district seems to have moved out of the orbit of the west, or 'Sikan', culture into that of the east, or 'Sikel', culture.

Similar observations apply in the case of Centuripe, a town which lies in a very strong position, controlling the valleys of the Symaithos, Kyamosoros (Salso) and Chrysas (Dittaino) rivers, right beside Etna. Here were found some tombs which from their looped fibulae with long curved pins must be regarded as being contemporary with Pantalica South, and dating therefore from about the eighth century B.C. Here, too, the associated pottery was always of the incised type closely related with Polizello and Sant' Angelo Muxaro. Examples of this incised pottery have been found as far afield as Paternò, on the southern slopes of Etna, though here, as we have already seen, they were found with typical products of the Pantalica-Cassibile-Finocchito style, and with elements showing contacts with the Italian mainland and the flourishing Ausonian culture of the Aeolian Islands. If, indeed, we are right in regarding the incised pottery of Sant' Angelo Muxaro style as the charac-teristic element of a cultural rather than of an ethnic *facies*, and identifiable with the Sikans, we should have to admit that these people must still have been living as far east as the Etna slopes even as late as the middle of the eighth century B.C.

To the north-west of the Sikans lay the territory of the Elymians, whose settlements were at Eryx and Segesta; while the coastal towns of Solunt, Panormos and Motya were in the hands of the Carthaginians. The most important of the material comes from Segesta. Here, unfortunately, we are only dealing with waste material without any chronological distinctions. Fragments of pottery painted with geometrical motifs are mixed with incised pottery in a style closely related to that of Sant' Angelo Muxaro, though in some respects different from it.

The most characteristic feature of this Elymian pottery is the stylized handle shaped like an animal's face; this does not seem to recur in the Agrigento district. The looped fibulae, and sometimes the stilted ones as well (both types always having a curved pin), are identical with those from Realmese and Pantalica South. We cannot, however, altogether rule out the possibility that in the central and western districts of Sicily, farther inland than the coastal zones where the Greeks founded their first colonies, there was a delay in the adoption of types imitating Greek ones, and that here in the west, fibulae of types extinct in eastern Sicily by about 730 B.C. lingered on in use until the end of the eighth or even well into the seventh century B.C.

Fig. 42

Elements related to those of Segesta have been found at Eryx and Motya as well as at Paceco in the Trapani province, and at San Giuseppe Iato, the ancient Iaetia, in the province of Palermo.

7. THE IRON AGE IN NORTH-EASTERN SICILY

To complete the picture of Sicily in the Early Iron Age, we should still take account of two small necropoleis discovered on the Tyrrhenian slopes of the province of Messina: one in the Uliveto countryside near Pozzo di Gotto, and the other at Rodì near Castroreale. Both belong to the Finocchito phase, are very similar to one another, and are separated by only a few kilometres. Both these necropoleis are composed of artificial rock-cut tombs, round or slightly squared, and though they have neither niches nor antechambers, they often have little side benches.

The pottery recovered from them is grey or blackish, and comprises only a few forms. Little globular jugs with high, narrow necks are the commonest form, and are decorated with horizontal wheel-made grooves or with finely incised geo-metrical motifs. Small amphorae, carinated cups, bowls, etc., were also found.

The fibulae are not very numerous and are either made of a small iron rod bound with thin bronze wire, or are of the four-spiralled type, by now showing Greek influence. There are ornamental bronze spirals, and Rodì also produced a little iron knife and spear-head.

There is an evident similarity to the Finocchito horizon, but there are no parallels in Sicily for the incised decoration on the pots. The closest analogies to this seem to come from the Calabrian necropoleis of Torre Galli and of the Locri district.

The difference between these two necropoleis and the near-by one of Milazzo is enormous, even though one of the chamber-tombs at Pozzo di Gotto produced a cinerary urn covered with its bowl, and identical with those from Milazzo: a curious, and at present unique, example of the mingling of two different rites and two different cultural worlds.

The habitation site belonging to the Pozzo di Gotto necro-polis has not been discovered, but the Rodì necropolis corre-sponds to the ancient Longane, a well-populated centre in a very strong position on the top of a small upland plateau, controlling the valley of the river of the same name. It was already in existence in the Early Bronze Age and survived until the fifth century B.C.

Traces of another habitation site of this period have recently been identified on the top of the steep Monte Scurzi, near Militello Rosmarino.

During this period there must have been founded all those strongly placed towns such as Longane, Abacaenum,

Aluntium, Apollonia which in Greek times we find scattered along the Tyrrhenian coast, and which were destined to be superseded by new towns founded by the Greeks in more favourable coastal sites, such as Alaesa, Calacte and Tyndaris. We might suppose that the maritime town of Agathyrnum, on the strength of legends which connected its foundation with the Aeolids of Lipari, may have been an overseas colony like Milazzo. But even the site of this town is uncertain today.

Somewhat different from the Tyrrhenian coastal necropoleis, though contemporary with them, is the small necropolis of Cocolonazzo di Mola, above Taormina, this time on the Ionian coast of the Messina province. This must correspond to a habitation site which existed on the crag now occupied by the hamlet of Castel Mola. Here, found with four-spiralled fibulae and little oinochoae analogous to the ones from Rodì and Pozzo di Gotto, was pottery painted in a geometrical style and different from that of south-eastern Sicily, though comparable to pottery from the Calabrian necropoleis in the Locri area (Canale, Ianchina and Patariti).

Like these Calabrian necropoleis, Cocolonazzo di Mola seems to show Greek influences which are not found on the Tyrrhenian coast.

8. SICILIAN BRONZE HOARDS

In following the course of Sicilian cultural evolution we have seen that metal was extremely rare, both in the Early and Middle Bronze Ages, while becoming gradually more and more diffused by the end of the Bronze Age and the beginning of the Iron Age, when it was widely employed in everyday life for personal ornamentation.

The museums in Sicily are rich in discoveries of this period, which corresponds to the cultural phase of Pantalica, Cassibile and Finocchito. Apart from the large numbers of objects found as grave-goods in the tombs, which have already been described, there is also a notable number of hoards and of isolated chance finds. These single objects, although brought to the museums individually, are often only elements of dismembered hoards.

Much discussion has taken place in the past as to the significance of hoards, which are regarded by some as sacred offerings to a divinity, and by others as hidden caches of founders or metal vendors.

As a matter of fact, right from very early times, perhaps from the time of its first diffusion, metal must, quite apart from its use in making implements, have served as a means of exchange. It is a reasonable supposition that in this capacity it took the place of the worked stone implements of earlier times. Metal used either in the raw or worked state for currency is the 'Aes rude' still remembered by the Romans, which had preceded the 'Aes signatum', the metal reduced to regular ingots and authorized by an official hall-mark. This, in its turn, was the precursor, at least on the Italian mainland, of the real and proper cast or coined money. This metal, then, either raw or made into implements, was the earliest money. The bronze hoards of this period have the same significance as the coin ones of a later date when money was beginning to be coined.

These bronze hoards often include some lumps or ingots of metal, but generally they are made up out of used objects, quite commonly broken or contorted. Sometimes they must have deliberately been broken to obtain the required metal weight for some particular exchange or to facilitate recasting.

Obviously, some of the types included amongst these out-of-date objects must already have been antiquated and have belonged to an earlier time than that of the hoard's burial; so the date of the burial is shown by the latest object contained in the group.

At other times the hoard may consist of unfinished objects which had never been used.

The large number of bronze axes of various types in Sicilian museums (Polizzello, Adrano, Paternò, etc.)—especially shaft-hole axes, which have never been sharpened and which still retain the casting jets and cannot therefore ever have been used either as implements or as weapons—clearly shows that they can only have had an exchange value.

So far, not one of the hoards found in Sicily has belonged to the Early or Middle Bronze Ages. Nor, so far, can any of them be attributed to the Pantalica North-Caltagirone period. The earliest hoards preserved in the Syracuse and Palermo museums cannot be dated before the Cassibile period.

Chronologically they can be divided into three big groups, the first of which corresponds to the Cassibile period, the second to the time of the Pantalica South cemetery, and the third to the Finocchito period.

Let us make a quick examination of the principal hoards, beginning with a list of the most significant pieces in each of them.

The Modica Hoard

This was found in 1898 at Mulino del Salto near Modica, and is now in the *Museo Preistorico* in Rome. It comprises:

One large shaft-hole axe (*e*) and two small examples of the same type.

Two flat axes with butts narrower than the blade, and with two little lateral projections (*i*).

Three socketed axes (*m*).

Two swords with T-shaped hilts, both with broken blades and very similar to one another. One of them is cast in one piece (*h*), and the other has the hilt fixed to the blade by rivets (*d*).

Three short leaf-shaped spears, perhaps for javelins or throwing spears (*k*).

A flame-shaped knife of the loop-handled type (*j*).

A broken razor (*c*).

A drill.

A saw (*l*).

A small cylindrical ornamental spiral (*b*).

A larger spiral of three coils (*a*).

Three simple arc fibulae, rather thickened (*f*).

Three stilted fibulae with rectilinear pin (*g*).

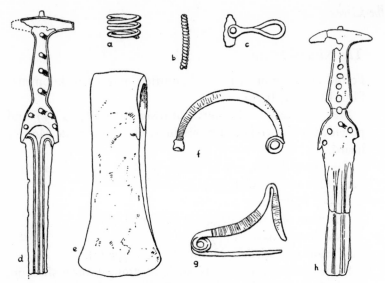

Fig. 43   Bronzes from the Modica hoard. Length of (e) 3¼", others to scale. Museo Preistorico, Rome.

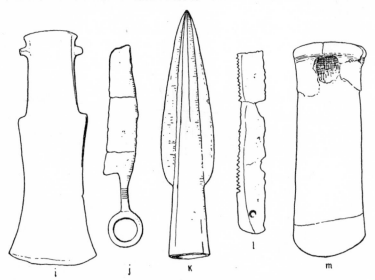

Fig. 44   Bronzes from the Modica hoard. Length of (k) 3⅞", others to scale. Museo Preistorico, Rome.

Fig. 46

The Niscemi Hoard

Found at Niscemi in the Gela district, only a few kilometres from Dessueri. It comprises:

Five flat axes with butts narrower than blades (*g*) and provided with two lateral projections, like those in the Modica hoard.

Two spear-heads, one of which has four protrusions at the base (*h*), and the other, two.

Sword fragment.

Fragment of a short dagger with riveted hilt (*j*).

Two riveted daggers (*f*).

A razor of Pantalica North-Dessueri type (*e*).

Some curious implements made of strong bronze sheeting, one hollowed inside and finger-nail-shaped (*c*), two others bent at right angles (*b, d*). One of these is shaped rather like a horse's head.

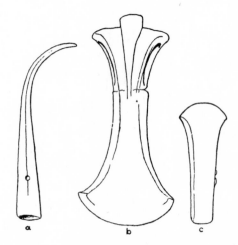

a   b   c

Fig. 45   Bronzes from the Malvagna hoard. Height of (c) $6\frac{1}{4}''$, *others to scale.*
Syracuse Museum.

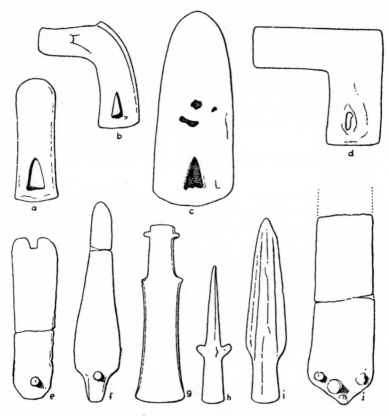

Fig. 46 Bronzes from the Niscemi hoard. Height of (b) 7⅔″, *others to scale. Syracuse Museum.*

The Malvagna (Messina) Hoard

Fig. 45

This consists of one flat axe (*c*) and three shaft-hole axes, one of which, ribbed and with a curved blade (*b*), is the best example of its type known from Sicily. With these was a curved spear (*a*), with a cylindrical socket and quadrangular section like the one from Niscemi.

Fig. 47

The Polizzello Hoard (*Mussomeli, province of Agrigento*)

Found near the mountain at Sant' Angelo Muxaro, one of the most important cultural centres in the west. Now in Palermo Museum. It comprises:

Three socketed axes, one of which has an incised hall-mark and is broken, and another still retaining the jets from casting (*a*).

Three axes, with square socket, one decorated with lines in relief (*c*).

An end wing axe (*b*).

Some spear fragments and ingots of bronze, etc.

The Monte San Mauro Hoard

Found on the site of the town of the same name as the hill near Caltagirone. Now in the Syracuse Museum.

This hoard consists of broken fragments of axes, and other objects. The axes include shaft-hole types and some square-
Fig. 47, c
socketed ones like those in the Polizzello hoard.

The Gratteri (*Cefalù*) Hoard (*now in the Palermo Museum*)

Contains eight flat axes, slightly flanged.

Two shaft-hole axes with bent tops.

One big ring.

Many of the elements in these hoards, like the stilted fibulae and the fibulae with thickened bow, the small loop-handled knives and the shaft-hole axes have been treated as characteristic types of the Cassibile period.

We have already stressed the fact that the Sicilian bronzes were often at this time typologically identical with those of the Iberian peninsula, the Atlantic coast of France and the British

Isles, while being basically different from the types diffused over the continent of Europe and the Italian mainland. It has been suggested here that these typological similarities with Iberia and the Atlantic coast between the tenth and eighth centuries B.C. may be attributed to the navigational activities of the Phoenicians.

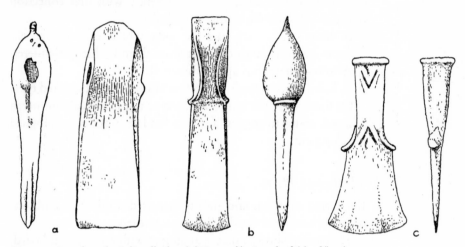

a   b   c

Fig. 47   Axes from the Polizzello hoard (Mussomeli). Length of (a) 2¾″, others to scale. Palermo Museum.

The bronze types common to Sicily and the west which are found in the necropoleis can be increased by others from the hoards. Examples include the flat axe with narrower butt than blade and side protrusions (Modica, Niscemi hoards and sporadic examples from Paternò, Caltagirone, Piazza Armerina, etc.), flat axes with wide, curved blade (Malvagna and Adrano hoards, and sporadic examples from Akrai, Giardini, Priolo, Licodia Eubea, Assoro, Cesarò, Leonforte, Etna, etc.), and socketed axes, some with widely curved blades (Malvagna hoard and other examples from Paternò, Piazza Armerina and Licodia Eubea).

SECOND GROUP

The Vizzini Hoard

Discovered in the country near Tre Canali, it passed into the collection of I. Cafici, and subsequently with that collection into the Syracuse Museum. It includes:

A long spear, very like the ones which characterize the Adrano hoard though differing from them by being slenderer.

Another analogous spear but smaller.

A little tanged dagger, and a few fibulae all of the stilted type.

Of these, only the long spear, a type not previously found in a hoard, seems to suggest a somewhat later stage of typological development.

The Lentini Hoard

Recovered in 1893, and mostly dispersed. Only a few objects have been secured for the Syracuse Museum.

This hoard shows notable analogies with the Vizzini hoard. It includes socketed spear-heads and one smaller spear much more like the Vizzini ones than those in the Adrano hoard (pp. 193–196); two rings and fragments of a third, and a few fragments of thick fibulae, not only of the stilted type as at Vizzini, but also of the somewhat later looped type.

The Santa Margherita Belice (Agrigento) Hoard

This group of thickened fibulae from Santa Margherita Belice should be referred to the same period as the Vizzini and Lentini groups.

One of them is of the stilted type called the Cassibile type, but the others have a curved pin. They are unusual variants of the type known from Pantalica South.

With these there was also an armlet made of many spirally coiled bronze strips like those which we shall find later in the Mendolito, Adrano and San Cataldo hoards.

THIRD GROUP

The hoards in the third group, while still containing some earlier objects, present on the whole the same types of objects as those found in the necropoleis of the Finocchito period, or

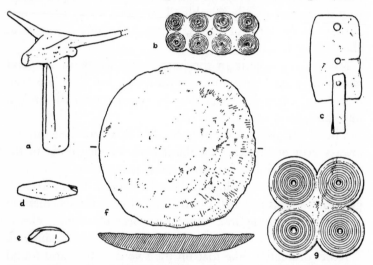

Fig. 48   Bronzes from the Mendolito di Adrano hoard. Length of (e) 3″, others to scale. Syracuse Museum.

which sometimes reappear in the earliest tombs of the Greek period. These include the long catch-plated fibulae, the ornamental chains, numerous rings, metal discs, etc.

The Adrano Hoard

This is by far the biggest of all the Sicilian hoards, since it weighs more than 15 cwt. It was found inside a large pithos,

Fig. 48

Plates 74, 77

on the site of a town whose name is not known and which is still largely unexplored in the Mendolito neighbourhood a few miles from the Graeco-Siculan Hadranum which was founded by Dionysus of Syracuse.

This hoard consists of a huge number of ingots, sometimes made into hollow spheres but generally unformed, many of which still contained objects (fibulae, bracelets, etc.) only partially melted. Evidently these out-of-use objects were being melted down into lumps of bronze of a desired weight which would be more readily saleable. This metal, either in the raw state or in the form of ingots, represented alone a weight of about 12 cwt.

Most of the objects in the hoard were weapons. A good twenty-nine are big complete spear-heads, but there are even more (144) examples of fragmentary ones, intentionally broken into three, four, or more pieces.

There was also a large number of big sword belts almost always bent or broken to make it easier to melt them in the crucible, but which, in many cases, it has been possible to straighten out again. Most of them have been decorated with geometric motifs in relief, but others still have the schematized anthropomorphic figures. One large piece of armour, clearly part of a warrior's breastplate, had a schematized face instead.

Relief decoration like that on the sword belts is also found on the greaves, though only a few fragments of these remain.

There was a large number of ornaments or objects of personal use, both whole or in fragments.

Fibulae were numerous, and except for a few examples still belonging to the Pantalica South type, were mostly of the long catch-plate variety, sometimes with a lozenge-shaped bow. Sometimes this was serpentine with side rods ending in studs of the type characteristic of the Finocchito period.

There were some beads of a biconical, somewhat elongated shape, and some strongly made plaques decorated with concen-

Plate 76

Plate 77

Plate 75

Plate 74

Fig. 48, d, e

tric circles, which in some cases suggest that they were imitating
cruciform four-spiral fibulae.

Fig. 48, b, g

Some razors of elongated quadrangular shape and with
small ribbon handles find their closest parallels with the tombs
at Sant' Angelo Muxaro and Polizzello in the Agrigento
district.

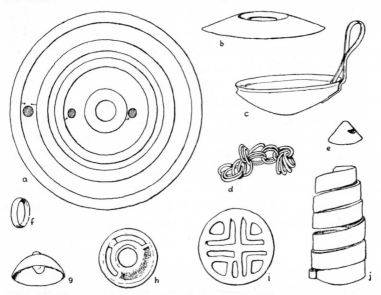

*Fig. 49   Bronzes from the San Cataldo (Caltagirone) hoard. Height of (j) 4¾″, others
to scale. Syracuse Museum.*

Numerous rings of bronze wire, varying in thickness from
about 1⅝ to 4¹⁵⁄₁₆ inches, all of them broken, or with a flattened
section, or else made from thin ribbon-like foil, large or small
hemispherical or conical bosses, big truncated conical bosses
with open tip, armlets made from spirally coiled bronze ribbon;
all of these belong to types which we shall see better represented
in the hoard of San Cataldo at Caltagirone.

Fig. 49, a, b, c,
g, j

In the latter hoard there are also dipper-cups made of bronze
foil, which are similar to the fragmentary specimens in the

Fig. 49, c

Fig. 50, a

Fig. 47, a
Fig. 41, h

Adrano hoard. Large basins or cauldrons of bronze sheeting with riveted joints were, rather incongruously, provided with cast handles almost identical to those which we shall find in the Giarratana hoard. Some stylized animal heads may have been part of the ornament on cauldrons or other bronze vessels, or possibly they may have been the tips of firedogs. Some big shaft-hole axes, one of which still retains the drippings from casting, a flat axe and a few small hollow cylinders of the characteristic Grammichele type seem to be typologically the earliest types in the hoard and to belong to a more ancient phase than all the rest of the material.

From its size the Mendolito hoard at Adrano seems to have constituted the treasure of the sanctuary or of a town, rather than the property of a private individual. It proves that bronze was worked on the spot and that out-of-use objects were scrapped and melted down into ingots. It raises again the same problem which confronted us when traces of a foundry were discovered in the Anaktoron at Pantalica: was metal-working at this period a princely monopoly or privilege?

Fig. 49

The Hoard of San Cataldo (near Caltagirone)

This large hoard, which belongs approximately to the same period as the Adrano hoard, was found at San Cataldo, in the Caltagirone territory, not far from the site of the anonymous Greek-Sikel town at Piano Casazzi, of which conspicuous stretches of walling are still left.

While the Adrano hoard consisted of an assemblage of objects of widely different types intended for melting, or already partly melted to make ingots, this San Cataldo hoard includes but few types of objects, most of them very much alike, and each group made up of a very large number of specimens, the majority of them being rings and bosses. The rings are very varied in size, with diameters ranging from $\frac{1}{2}$ to $2\frac{5}{16}$ inches.

They are generally made of cylindrical wire *(a)*, sometimes flattened in section and occasionally ribbon-shaped *(f)*.

The bosses are sometimes bowl-shaped and sometimes conical *(g, e)*, with an inner ring or a small hole on the tip; sometimes they are wider and like a truncated cone open at the tip *(b)*. Besides these, there are some discoidal ornamental pendants

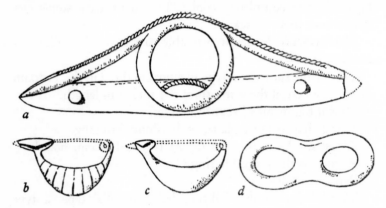

Fig. 50   Bronzes from the Giarratana hoard. Length of largest object 7¼", others to scale. Syracuse Museum.

with circles either arranged concentrically or enclosing a cross decoration *(h, i)*, several little chains *(d)*, three armlets of wide spirally coiled bronze ribbon *(j)*, a flattened disc-shaped spiral, perhaps belonging to a large fibula, and three little bronze bowls, two of which have high dipper-shaped handles *(c)*.

With the exception of the ornamental disc *(h, i)* and the flattened disc-shaped spiral, all the types found in this hoard recur again in the Adrano hoard with which there is therefore a perfect correspondence.

The homogeneity of the objects constituting the San Cataldo hoard, and the perfect state of their efficiency, lead one to wonder whether this is in fact a true founder's hoard, i.e. a stock of goods just produced or, at least, intended for sale.

Fig. 50

The Giarratana Hoard

Found in 1892 in the Donna Scala neighbourhood, this contained no less than 440 pounds of metal ingots or lumps. Some of the ingots seem to have been produced by pouring the melted metal into a large flat pan, and cutting it up into sections before it was completely cool. These slabs were sometimes almost four inches thick.

The Syracuse Museum was able to recover the following items:

Plate 76

Three large spears of a type identical to those in the Adrano hoard; the best of them measures 22¼ inches in length.

Several fragments of shaft-hole axes.

A leaf-shaped knife-blade, with a long thin tang.

Figs. 45, a; 46, h

A spit similar to those in the Malvagna-Niscemi hoards.

A curious thick double ring *(d)*.

Part of a fibula.

Two fibulae of the full-rounded 'navicella' type, a type altogether foreign to Sicily, though proper to central Italy *(b, c)*.

A handle belonging to a great cauldron similar to those in the Adrano hoard *(a)*.

This hoard too, then, is markedly similar to the Adrano one, though containing some typologically earlier objects (the spit), or exotic ones (fibulae of the 'navicella' type).

Plate 78

A Collection of Bronzes from the Noto Hills

In 1916 the Syracuse Museum purchased a collection of bronzes. It was impossible to ascertain the circumstances of their discovery, though the bronzes were known to come from the hills near Noto (Syracuse), probably from Noto Vecchio, Tremenzano and Finocchito. Orsi thought they were found by clandestine excavations in a necropolis, but more probably they were the very rich grave-goods of one or more tombs.

Most of the items seem to be the ornamental outfit of one individual, possibly the chief of some indigenous tribe, laid out with barbaric sumptuousness. Ornamental objects made with bronze wire spirals are the commonest type.

Ten cylindrical or slightly conical spirals must have been worn on the fingers of both hands, since some phalanges are still sticking to the metal through its oxidization. Two larger cylindrical spirals must have encircled the forearms. A large group of tubular spirals, each of about $\frac{11}{16}$ of an inch in diameter and with a total length of about $37\frac{3}{8}$ inches, were perhaps part of one or two long necklaces. Less clear is the significance of other small cylindrical spirals some $\frac{1}{4}$ of an inch in diameter and $\frac{3}{8}$ of an inch in length. Thirty-four small hemispherical bosses with inner rings may have been buttons of the dress. This collection also includes: three torques of thin twisted wire with coiled ends; a huge cruciform fibula made with four disc-shaped spirals, one of which is missing; other disc-shaped spirals, perhaps odd pieces of analogous fibulae of the same size or smaller; two little ornamental spirals in the shape of spectacles, and three in the shape of a biconical bead; some large bracelets, each of them made with a few coils of wire, with several rings threaded on it; a large group of bronze-foil rings of various diameters (from $\frac{3}{4}$ to $2\frac{9}{16}$ inches), and a number of smaller rings made of thin round or flat-sectioned wire; several small ornamental chains, discoid pendants with concentric circles, etc. There were also some large fibulae, three of which were of the characteristic Pantalica South type with looped and curved pins, whereas other fragmentary ones with thickened bow, or with ribbon or stilted bow, are the earliest items from the collection.

There is also a two-piece fibula, with pins revolving around the bow, of a type very rare in Sicily, but which, as we have already said, has parallels both in the east (Crete) and in the Iberian peninsula (Huerta de Arriba), etc.

While the looped or curved-pin fibulae take us back to the period of Pantalica South, many of the other items, such as the four-spiral fibulae, the spirals and the ornamental chains, the large number of discs and rings, have parallels in the Finocchito period tombs and in the hoards contemporaneous with them, such as those at Adrano, San Cataldo and Giarratana.

Practical Information

Almost all the prehistoric material from Sicily can be found in the three big national museums at Syracuse, Palermo and Lipari. The *Museo Eoliano* at Lipari has all the finds from the Aeolian Islands and from Milazzo, and provisionally houses material from the near/by coast of Sicily. At Palermo there is most of the palaeolithic material and also of the western Sicilian pottery (Conca d'Oro culture type, West Castelluccio, etc.). In the *Museo Nazionale* at Syracuse there are most of the discoveries from eastern Sicily, as well as central and southern Sicily (including the sites in the Agrigento region, such as Serraferlicchio, Montedoro, Caldare, Sant' Angelo Muxaro, Polizzello, etc.). The other local museums in Sicily—at Trapani, Termini Imerese, Cefalù, Agri/gento, Gela and Catania—only contain a small amount of prehistoric material.

Since the collections of Barons Corrado and Ippolito Cafici were bequeathed or presented to the Syracuse Museum, no other private prehistoric collections remain in the island, and there is very scanty Sicilian material to be found outside Sicily.

Visitors to the palaeolithic caves in the Palermo neighbourhood (Addaura, Grotta Niscemi) should apply to the *Soprintendenza alle Antichità*, which has its offices in the *Museo Nazionale* in Palermo. To the same *Soprintendenza* they should apply for the Grotta della Cala dei Genovesi in the island of Levanzo, which is reached by boat leaving from Trapani three times a week.

The Bronze Age villages in the islands of Panarea and Filicudi (those at Salina have been filled in) can be reached by the boat plying between these islands and Lipari (see the official Italian State Railways time/table for the Aeolian and Egadi Islands).

The great necropoleis in the Syracuse neighbourhood (Castelluccio, Melilli, Thapsos and Plemmyrion, Cozzo del Pantano, Cassibile, Pantalica, Palazzolo Acreide, Finocchito, etc.) can· be visited by car on a one/day excursion; there is, as a rule, no possibility of finding accommodation on the spot.

Information may be obtained from the *Soprintendenza alle Antichità della Sicilia Orientale*, whose offices are in the *Museo Nazionale* at Syracuse, and from the *Ispettori onorari alle Antichità* in the main archaeological centres in Sicily.

The Dessueri necropolis can be visited from Gela. Information about antiquities in the Agrigento and Caltanissetta provinces may be obtained from the *Soprintendenza alle Antichità* at Agrigento, or from the *Museo Archeologico* at Gela.

Short Bibliography

General Works

F. VON ANDRIAN, *Prähistorische Studien aus Sizilien*, Supplement to 'Zeitschrift für Ethnologie', X, Berlin, 1878.

G. A. COLINI, *La Civiltà del Bronzo in Sicilia*, in 'Bollettino di Paletnologia Italiana', XXX, 1904, pp. 115, 211, 229; XXXI, 1905, p. 18.

T. E. PEET, *The Stone and Bronze Ages in Italy and Sicily*, Oxford, 1909.

C. & I. CAFICI, in EBERT, 'Reallexikon der Vorgeschichte', 1925–28. *See under Sikuler, Sizilien B. Jüngere Perioden, Cannatello, Isnello-Kultur, Monte Tabuto, Pantalica, Stentinello-Kultur.*

G. PATRONI, *La Preistoria*, Vallardi, Milano, 1937.

B. PACE, *Arte e Civiltà della Sicilia Antica*, vol. I, 1935; vol. II, 1938.

L. BERNABÒ BREA, *Gli Scavi nella caverna delle Arene Candide (Finale Ligure)*, 'Istituto Internazionale di Studi Liguri, Bordighera', vol. I, 1946; vol. II, 1956.

L. BERNABÒ BREA, *La Sicilia prehistorica y sus relaciones con Oriente y con la Peninsula Ibérica*, in 'Ampurias', XV–XVI, Barcelona, 1953–54.

L. BERNABÒ BREA & M. CAVALIER, *Civiltà preistoriche delle Isole Eolie e del territorio di Milazzo*, in 'Bollettino di Paletnologia Italiana', LXV, 1956.

The Palaeolithic

R. VAUFREY, *Le Paléolitique Italien*, in 'Archives de l'Institut de Paléon-tologie Humaine', Mémoire 3, Paris, 1928.

R. VAUFREY, *Les Eléphants nains des Iles Méditerranéennes*, ibid., Mémoire 6, Paris, 1929.

C. MAVIGLIA, 'Archivio per l'Antropologia e la Etnologia', LXX, 1940, p. 95; LXXI, 1941, p. 90 (Grotta S. Teodoro).

L. BERNABÒ BREA, 'Ampurias', XI, Barcelona, 1949, p. 1 (Grotta Corruggi); XII, p. 19, *Palaeolithic Stations of South-east Sicily*.

P. GRAZIOSI, 'Rivista di Scienze Preistoriche', V, 1950, p. 1; VIII, 1953, p. 123; IX, 1954, p. 79 (Levanzo).

I. MARCONI BOVIO, 'Bollettino di Paletnologia Italiana', 1953, p. 5; and 'Bollettino d'Arte del Ministero della Pubblica Istruzione', XXXVI, 1953, pp. 61–68 (Addaura).

I. MARCONI BOVIO, 'Bollettino di Paletnologia Italiana', LXIV, 1954–55, p. 57 (Grotta Niscemi).

P. GRAZIOSI, *L'Arte dell' antica età della pietra*, Sansoni, Florence, 1956, pl. 286–300.

The Neolithic and the Copper Age

C. CAFICI, *Stazioni preistoriche di Trefontane e Poggio Rosso in territorio di Paternò*; in 'Monumenti Antichi dei Lincei', XXIII, 1915.

C. CAFICI, *La stazione neolitica di Fontana di Pepe*, in 'Atti della Acca-demia di Scienze e Lettere di Palermo', XII, 1920.

P. ORSI, *Megara Hyblaea; Villaggio neolitico e tempio greco e di taluni singo-larissimi vasi di Paternò*, in 'Monumenti Antichi dei Lincei', XXVII, 1921.

P. E. ARIAS, *La stazione preistorica di Serraferlicchio presso Agrigento*, ibid., XXXVI, 1938.

I. MARCONI BOVIO, *La cultura tipo Conca d'Oro della Sicilia Nord-Occidentale*, ibid., XL, 1944.

The Bronze Age and the Iron Age

P. ORSI, *Necropoli Sicula presso Siracusa con vasi e bronzi micenei* (*Cozzo Pantano*), in 'Monumenti Antichi dei Lincei', II, 1893.

P. ORSI, *Thapsos*, ibid., VI, 1895.

P. ORSI, *Pantalica e Cassibile*, ibid., IX, 1899.

A. MOSSO, *Villaggi preistorici di Caldare e Cannatello presso Agrigento*, in 'Monumenti Antichi dei Lincei', XVIII, 1908.

P. ORSI, *Necropoli sicule di Pantalica e Monte Dessueri*, ibid., XXI, 1913.

P. ORSI, *Le necropoli preelleniche calabresi di Torre Galli e di Canale Ianchina, Patariti*, ibid., XXXI, 1926.

P. MINGAZZINI, *Due tombe sicule in territorio di Partanna presso Selinunte*, in 'Studi di Archeologia e Arte editi dalla Società P. Orsi', I, Milano, 1939, pp. 47 ff.

P. GRIFFO, *Ricerche intorno al sito di Camico*, in 'Studi Siciliani di Archeologia e Storia Antica', 2; Agrigento, 1948.

I. MARCONI BOVIO, *El problema des los Elimos a la luz de descubrimientos recientes*, in 'Ampurias', XII, 1950, p. 79.

L. BERNABÒ BREA, *Villaggio dell'età del bronzo nell'isola di Panarea*, in 'Bollettino d'Arte del Ministero della Pubblica Istruzione', 1951, p. 31.

L. BERNABÒ BREA, *Segni grafici e contrassegni sulle ceramiche dell'età del Bronzo delle Isole Eolie*, 'Minos', II, 1952.

L. BERNABÒ BREA, *Akrai*, Catania, 1956.

See particularly the long series of articles published by Paolo Orsi almost every year in the 'Bollettino di Paletnologia Italiana' from 1889 to 1937:

XV, 1889, p. 48 (Siracusa); XVI, 1890, p. 177 (Stentinello); XVII, 1897, pp. 53, 115 (Melilli-Plemmirion); XVIII, 1892, pp. 1, 67 (Castelluccio); XIX, 1893, p. 30 (idem); XX, 1894, p. 37 (Finocchito); XXI, 1895, p. 80 (Agrigento); XXIII, 1897, pp. 1, 105 (Agrigento); ibid., p. 157 (Finocchito); XXIV, 1898, p. 165 (Monte Tabuto); XXVI, 1900, pp. 164, 267

(Bronze hoards from Giarratana, Lentini, Mineo and Grammichele); XXVIII–XXIX, 1902–3, pp. 103, 23, 136 (Valsavoia, Rivettazzo, Matrensa); XXXI, 1905, p. 96 (Molino della Badia); XXXIII, 1907, p. 7 (Calafarina, Barriera); XXXIV, 1908, pp. 119, 155 (Piano Notaro); XXXVI, 1911, p. 158 (Branco Grande, Sette Farine); XXXIX, 1914, p. 92 (Centuripe); XLI, 1915, p. 71 (Pozzo di Gotto); XLIII, 1923, p. 3 (Comiso); XLVI, 1926, p. 5 (Sante Croci); XLVII, 1927, p. 35 (Bronze hoards from Niscemi, San Cataldo, Caltagirone, and Malvagna); XLVIII, 1928, p. 44 (Serraferlicchio, Naro, Palma Montechiaro, Bersaglio di Caltagirone, Lipari); L–LI, 1930–31, p. 134 (Biancavilla).

See also 'Notizie degli Scavi di Antichità'; 1898, p. 222 (Barriera); 1899, p. 69 (Melilli); 1904, p. 65 (Caltagirone); 1919, p. 360 (Taormina); 'Archivio Storico Siciliano', 1893, p. 308 (Cava Secchiera, Molinello); 'Atti della Accademia di Scienze e Lettere di Palermo', 1932 p. 18 (Sant' Angelo Muxaro).

SOURCES OF ILLUSTRATIONS

The photographs for the plates, except where otherwise specified, were taken by Signor Salvatore Fontana of the Syracuse Museum.

The figures are either old drawings reproduced from the publications of Paolo Orsi or were drawn by Professor Oreste Puzzo and Signor Uberto Lazzarini of the Syracuse Museum. Where not drawn from the originals, their sources are as follows: Figures 1, 2, Graziosi, *Rivista di Scienze Preistoriche*; 3, Marconi Bovio, *Bollettino di Paletnologia Italiana*; 12, 16, 17, Marconi Bovio, *Conca d'Oro*; 21, *Atti Congresso Preistorico e Protcistorico Mediterraneo* and *Reallexikon der Vorgeschichte*; 32–34, 37 (*g*), 39, Orsi, *Monumenti Antichi dei Lincei*; 35 (2 and 4), Pericot, *Historia de Espana*; 35 (6 and 18), Martinez Santa Olalla; 35 (14), 42, *Ampurias* (Barcelona); 35 (17), Montelius; 38, 41, 43–46, 49, 50, *Bolletino di Paletnologia Italiana*; 47, Gabrici, *Atti della Accademia di Scienze e Lettere di Palermo*.

The maps were drawn by J. Woodcock and (except for No. I) are based on originals supplied by the Soprintendenza alle Antichità della Sicilia Orientale, Syracuse.

THE PLATES

2

6

7

8

9

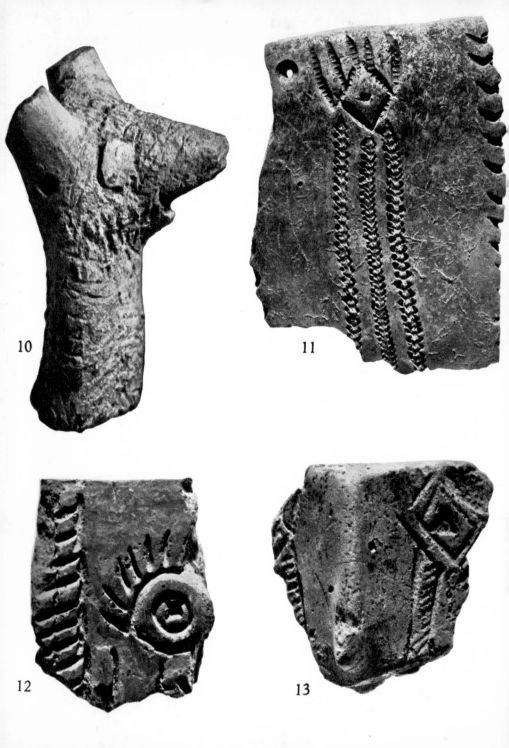

10   11

12   13

14

15

16

17

18

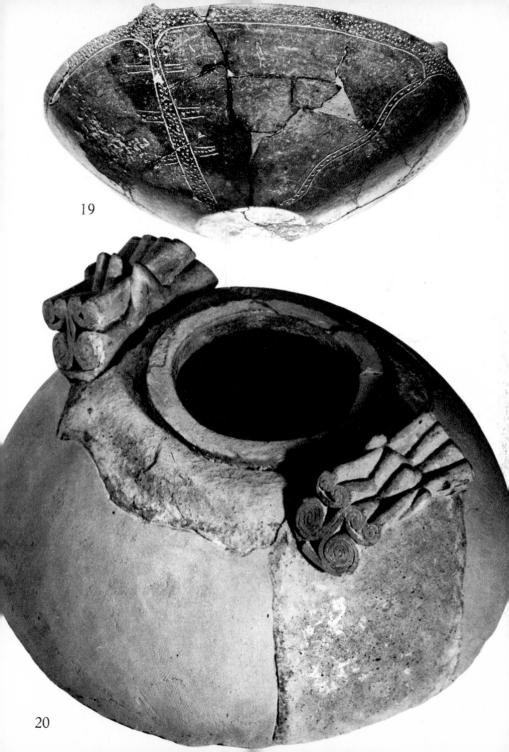

19

20

21

22

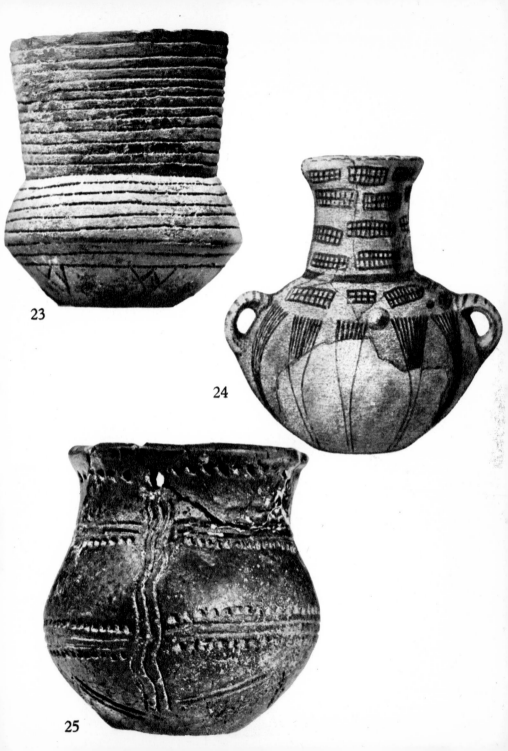

23

24

25

26

27

28

29

30

31

32

33

34

35

36

37

38

39

40

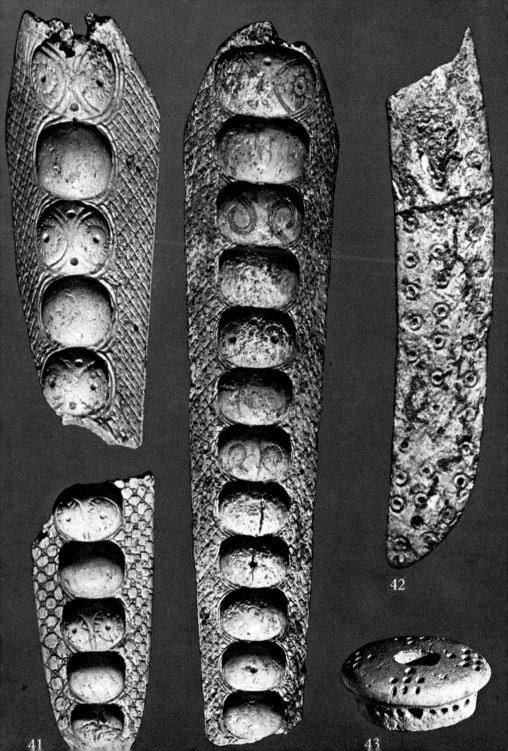

41

42

43

44

45

46

47

48

49

51

52

53

54

55

56

57

58

59

60

62

63

65

66

67

68

69

70

72

71

73

74

75

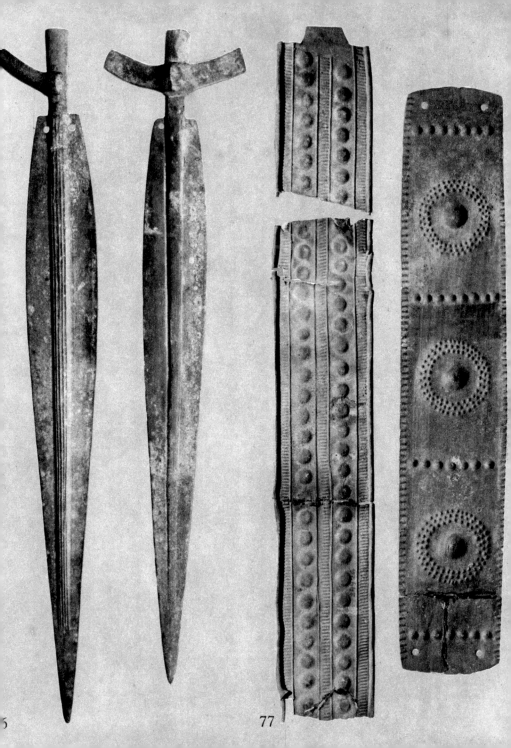

77

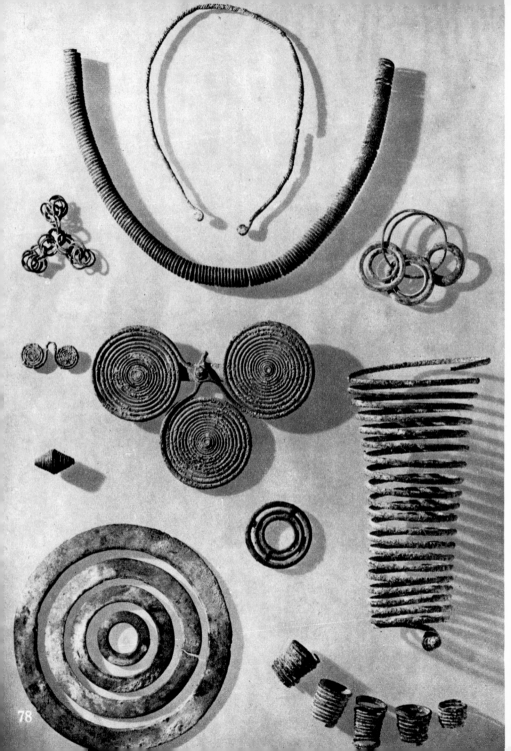

Notes on the Plates

1   Levanzo, Grotta dei Genovesi. Young deer. (Photo: P. Graziosi.) Height of figure 7⅞ in.

, 3   Levanzo, Grotta dei Genovesi.

2   Schematized human or animal figures painted in black. (Photo: Kirner, Palermo.) Height of painted flash about 2 ft. 7½ in.

3   Little seated figure painted in red. (Photo: F. Teegen, Hamburg.) Height about 1 ft.

4   Grotta dell'Addaura:
Ritual dance, incised deeply on the rock. (Photo: Soprintendenza Antichitá, Palermo.) The man in the centre is 9½ in. high.

5   Grotta dell'Addaura:
Hunter and fallow deer; deep incision of the second group. The deer is 1 ft. high.
On the left: a woman with a bundle, belonging to the earliest group. (Photo: Soprintendenza Antichitá, Palermo.)

, 7   Neolithic pottery in the Stentinello style.

6   Vase from Naxos (Messina). Diameter at mouth 8½ in.

7   Flask from Matrensa (Syracuse). Height 7½ in.

, 9   Neolithic pottery in the Stentinello style.

8   Pot from Stentinello. Diameter at mouth 5⅞ in.

9   Pot from Matrensa. Diameter at mouth 5½ in.

10–15 The Stentinello culture.

10 Head of a dog from Stentinello. Height just over 2 in.

11, 12, 13 Fragments of pots with stylized eyes, and in the shape ot human faces, from Trefontane. Height of largest fragment about 4 in.

14 Pot with a human face from Trefontane. Height just over 2 in.

15 Cup painted with black-bordered red flames, from Megara Hyblaea (from a water-colour by Rosario Carta). Diameter 7½ in.

16, 17 Pottery painted with bands or flames coloured red and edged with black, from the lower levels of the Lipari acropolis phase II of the Aeolian Neolithic. Lipari Museum. Height of biggest six-handled vase 8½ in.

18, 19 Decorated vases from the tombs on the Iozza estate at Piano Notaro (Gela). Diameter of the big bowl 11 in.

20 Scroll-handled vase from Paternó. Syracuse Museum. Maximum girth just under 11 in.

21, 22 Burnished decorated pottery of the Sicilian Copper Age.

21 Trefontane (Paternó). Diameter 7 in.

22 Grotta della Chiusazza (Syracuse). Height 6¾ in.

23 Local imitation of a bell-beaker in the Moarda style, from Torrebigini (Selinunte). From a water-colour by Rosario Carta. Height 4¾ in.

24 Painted pottery of the Serraferlicchio style (Serraferlicchio). From a water-colour by Rosario Carta. Height of flash on left 9¼ in.

25 A beaker from Carini, decorated in the Conca d'Oro style. Syracuse Museum. Height 3⅜ in.

26, 27 Pottery of the Moarda style.

26 Pot from Villafrati. Height 3½ in., diam. 4½ in.

27 Pot from Moarda. Height 8 in.

, 29 Pots in the Castelluccio style, from Monte Sallia. Height of one-handled vase 5 in.

30 Early Mycenaean pottery from the Bronze Age levels of the Lipari Acropolis. Height of handled fragment 2¾ in.

31 The island of Filicudi with the site of the Bronze Age village on the Capo Graziano promontory on the left. (Photo: G. Costa, Lipari.)

32 Huts in the Bronze Age village of Capo Graziano (Filicudi).

33 Carved door-slab from the Castelluccio rock-cut tombs. Syracuse Museum.

34 Flint mines later used as burial places, at Monte Tabuto (Comiso).

, 37 Rock-cut tombs at Cava Lazzaro. (Photo: G. Scichilone.) Length of antechamber shown in Fig. 35, 11 ft. 6 in.; height 3 ft.

36 Rock-cut tomb with a four-pillared antechamber in the Castelluccio necropolis (Noto). Height of pilasters 4 ft. 3 in.; length of antechamber 15 ft. 9 in.

, 39 Painted pottery of West Castelluccio style.

38 Pot from Monte Aperto. Syracuse Museum. Height 13¾ in.

39 Pot from Monte Aperto. Agrigento Museum.

40 Painted pot of Castelluccio style from Monte Tabuto (Comiso).

41 Bossed bone objects from the tombs at Cava della Signora (Castelluccio). Height of biggest 6½ in.

42 Bone plaque decorated with dotted circles from Melilli. Length 2¾ in.

43 Bone sword pommel from Monte Sallia tomb IX. Length about 1½ in.

44 The Milazzese promontory in the island of Panarea.

45, 46 Huts of the Bronze Age village on the Milazzese promontory in the island of Panarea.

47 Round hut (A) of the Bronze Age village at La Portella in the island of Salina. Internal diameter 9 ft. 10 in.

48 Vase in the Milazzese style from the Middle Bronze Age levels of the Lipari acropolis. Height 15¾ in.

49 Pithos burials in the Middle Bronze Age necropolis at Milazzo.

50 Vase in the Milazzese style from the Middle Bronze Age necropolis at Milazzo.

51 Middle Bronze Age rock-cut tomb in the Thapsos necropolis.

52 Collapsed rock-cut tombs in the Thapsos necropolis.

53 Cinerary situlae and pithoi: burials in the Early Iron Age necropolis of Lipari.

54 Tomb 115 in the Milazzo urn-field.

55 Ivory comb and imported Mycenaean faience beads from the Plemmyrion necropolis. Length of comb 2⅛ in.

56 Gold ring with prophylactic eye-decoration from Caltagirone.

57 Gold ring with fish decoration from Pantalica. Diameter 0·67 in. (1·7 cm.)

58 Gold ring decorated with plaited pattern from Pantalica.

60 Mycenaean pottery from the Bronze Age necropoleis in the Syracuse district.

    59 Pot from Matrensa. Height $7\frac{1}{8}$ in.

    60 Jug from Thapsos, tomb 37. Height $4\frac{3}{8}$ in.

61 High-footed vase of monochrome red ware from Pantalica. Height 3 ft. $6\frac{1}{2}$ in.

62 Cup painted with bird-figures from Lentini. Height $2\frac{3}{4}$ in.

63 Incised basin of grey ware from Modica. Height $7\frac{1}{4}$ in. Diameter 13 in.

64 Pantalica, the north necropolis. (Photo: G. Scichilone.)

65 The Anaktoron at Pantalica. (Photo: Maltese, Syracuse.) Length in front 38 ft.

66 Tomb in the Cassibile necropolis.

68 Lentini, remains of rectangular huts on the Meta Piccola Hill. (Photo: G. Rizza.)

69 The necropolis of Cozzo San Giuseppe at Realmese, near Calascibetta (Enna).

—73 The Early Iron Age in the Agrigento district.

    70, 71 Painted oinochoae from the Agrigento district. Height of largest $9\frac{7}{8}$ in.

    72 Gold rings from Sant' Angelo Muxaro. Diameter of setting $1\frac{3}{8}$ in. (3·5 cm.). Weight 54·8 grammes.

    73 Askos with impressed decoration from tomb 9 at Polizzello. Height $6\frac{1}{2}$ in.

74, 75 Bronze hoard from Mendolito, near Adrano (Etna).

    74 Fragment of greave. Length 7 in.

    75 Schematized human face on bronze foil. Measurements $5\frac{7}{8}$ by 4 in.

76, 77 Bronze hoard from Mendolito, near Adrano (Etna).

    76 Spear-heads. Length of biggest $22\frac{7}{8}$ in.

    77 Belts. Length of biggest $16\frac{7}{8}$ in.

    78 Collection of bronzes from the Noto hills, perhaps the grave goods from a tomb. Length of Spiral armlet $8\frac{5}{8}$ in.

Index